UZBEK

Uzbek–English
English–Uzbek

Dictionary
&
Phrasebook

Nicholas Awde,
William Dirks, &
Umida Hikmatullaeva

T0275360

HIPPOCRENE BOOKS, INC.
New York

Thanks to . . . Fred James Hill
and Caroline Gates
for their help in compiling
this volume.

———◆———

Typeset & designed by Desert♥Hearts

ISBN 0 7818 0959 2

For information, address:
HIPPOCRENE BOOKS, INC.
171 Madison Avenue
New York, NY 10016
www.hippocrenebooks.com

Printed in the United States of America

CONTENTS

- An Uzbek person is an **o'zbek**.
- The adjective for Uzbek is **o'zbek**.
- Uzbeks call themselves **o'zbeklar**.
- The Uzbek language is **o'zbekcha**.
- Uzbekistan is **O'zbekistan**.

INTRODUCTION

From their unique vantage point at the center of the legendary Silk Road between China and Europe, the fabled cities and towns of Uzbekistan grew to become key links whose influence, wealth and fame stretched far beyond the line of this ancient trading route — the mere mention of Samarqand and Bukhara conjures images of gleaming minarets and golden-roofed markets.

Indeed, Uzbekistan is a major hub for the entire region of Central Asia — a position it has held for centuries — and its most populous nation. In its present form the country emerged only as a single unified entity in the early 20th century — prior to this, the region was part of an ever-changing political landscape that was continually embroiled in the ambitious designs of a host of different khanates and empires.

Land of the khanates

The region began to make its way into written history with the arrival of the Achaemenids, a hugely influential Persian dynasty, founded by Cyrus the Great in the 6th century B.C. The first ruler in history to take the title of 'shah' or 'lord', Cyrus's empire was huge even by today's standards, encompassing lands from the Aegean Sea to present-day Pakistan.

The realm he left to his descendants was famously toppled by Alexander the Great a few centuries later in 331 B.C., who subsequently stormed into Central Asia in pursuit of his own imperial ambitions. The Macedonian commander spent time in Samarqand in order to deal with a rebellious faction of his army. Later, in 327 B.C., while chasing his enemies east of the city, he fell for the charms of the princess Roxana, daughter of a local chieftain and whisked her southwards to Bactria, in present-day Afghanistan, to marry her.

On Alexander's death, the immense lands he had conquered were carved up between his generals, and the region of Uzbekistan was integrated into a new empire ruled by the Greek Seleucid dynasty. During this period strong links of culture and trade were developed between East and West through the territories of Uzbekistan. Later, under the Buddhist Kushan dynasty, which came to power in the first century B.C., Uzbekistan flourished as never before when the Silk Road came into full bloom.

The golden age of Islam

The region subsequently underwent several drastic changes of hand as the Zoroastrian kingdom of the Persian Sassanians from the south, and the Huns and later Turkish nomads from the east, staked their claims on the region. It was the latter who, in the 6th century, brought a large part of Central Asia under their control and settled in large numbers among the local peoples they had conquered.

Uzbekistan's rich Islamic heritage began with the arrival of the Arabs, who incorporated the region into their empire during the 8th century. Although these latest arrivals also came to lose their grip on the region, their religion had found fertile ground in which to take root. By the 9th century, Bukhara had blossomed into a major center of Islamic learning, enjoying a reputation that was to spread throughout Central Asia, Persia and beyond. Today Bukhara along with Samarqand and Khiva boast some of the finest examples of Islamic architecture in the world.

The region suffered ravages of the ubiquitous Mongols under Genghis Khan in the 13th century, but in the following century, it gained a new lease of life under the ferocious leader Timur, a Muslim Turk. Fired by his ambitions to control the lucrative East-West trade routes, Timur carved himself out a huge empire that at its peak stretched from Turkey to India.

Moving westwards — in the opposite direction to his predecessor Alexander — the great Mongol commander made Samarqand the capital of his new Timurid Empire and transformed it into one of the greatest cities the world had ever seen. Under Timur and his successors, architecture, literature and the sciences flourished. Timur's own grandson Ulugh Beg was one of the finest astronomers the world had seen, and oversaw the construction of a magnificent observatory in the capital.

It was also under the Timurids that the legendary 15th-century poet and statesman Ali Shir Nava'i thrived. One of Uzbekistan's best known figures and a giant in the world of Persian literature, his work also popularized the Turkish literary language of Chagatai, the precursor to modern literary Uzbek.

Rise of the Uzbeks

Timurid rule came to an end with the ascendancy of the Uzbeks in the early 15th century. The Uzbek Turks took their name from the 14th century khan Öz Beg, the greatest ruler of the huge western part of the Mongol Empire known as the Golden Horde.

A convert to Islam, Öz Beg did much to bring about the Islamification of his empire. In time, the descendants of Muslim Turks loyal to the great khan moved south and established themselves firmly in Central Asia. By the mid-15th century, the Uzbeks had established the two khanates of Bukhara and Khiva.

It was the intermingling of these Turks with the inhabitants of the region (which included various other Turkic groups and the Persian-speaking Tajiks) that gave rise to the modernday Uzbek language. Today, Uzbek is by no means limited to Uzbekistan itself but is also spoken by millions of others in the neighboring countries of Tajikistan, Kyrgyzstan, Afghanistan, and Kazakhstan.

Despite being shaken by a Persian invasion in the mid-18th century, led by its ambitious ruler Nadir Shah, the Uzbek khanates managed to survive. However, a division in Bukhara led to the emergence of a third breakaway khanate, Kokand. Centered on the mountainous Fergana Valley to the east, Kokand also took in the territory of the neighboring Kyrgyz people, also Turks.

But overall, there was little uniformity across the region. With a wide array of peoples and their various clans in the region, the trio of khanates were far from clearly defined territorial states and their rulers had no shortage of unruly local chieftains to contend with internally — who fiercely defended the rights of their own clans and families.

The Russian conquest

A new era in Uzbek history began in the 19th century, as Central Asia became caught up in the so-called 'Great Game' that turned the region into an arena for competing imperial ambitions — principally those of Great Britain and Russia. Flush with its successful expansion into the Caucasus, the Tsar's armies launched a vigorous campaign in the 1860s and by the mid-1870s, the three khans of Bukhara, Khiva and Kokand were finally forced to accept Russian domination. The last vestiges of the khanates were finally eliminated in the aftermath of the Russian Revolution and the birth of the Soviet Union.

Once in power, the Soviets began their masterplan to divide the peoples of Central Asia — as elsewhere in the new union — into territorial units based on ethnicity. As part of the plan, the Soviet Socialist Republic of Uzbekistan was formally created in 1924.

Uzbek became the official language of the new republic, and the Soviet authorities busied themselves crafting a standard language using Chagatai and elements from the various dialects, as well as a liberal dosage of Soviet, Russian ("international") vocabulary.

Yet, in reality, the republic was by no means homogeneous and it contained significant numbers of non-Uzbek minorities within its borders. While more than three-quarters of the population is Uzbek, there are also significant minorities including Tajiks, Kazaks, Russians, Kyrgyz, Tatars, and Koreans. Conversely, sizeable numbers of Uzbeks reside in the countries that surround Uzbekistan.

Dawn of independence

After seven decades of harsh Soviet rule, the people of Uzbekistan finally achieved their independence in August 1991, yet the transition to international statehood in the last decade of the 20th century was far from easy. The previous 80 years had left a legacy of social and political problems that Uzbekistan is still in the process of overcoming. In particular, the grand Soviet scheme to reel in Central Asian cotton had channeled much of the republic's agricultural resources into large-scale cotton cultivation, making it one of the top producers in the world — the fields were famously among the few man-made features of the earth visible from outer space. Yet the extensive irrigation needed to support the industry contributed to huge environmental problems that led to the severe contraction and ruin of the Aral Sea, one of the world's largest lakes.

Despite the trials of the recent past, the people of Uzbekistan have stepped into the 21st century with their spirit and strong sense of historical identity intact. Blessed with a country rich in natural resources — including gas, oil, gold, and other metals — the Uzbeks have now begun to take control over their own destiny, enabling them to put not just Uzbekistan, but Central Asia too, squarely on the map once more. ■

Further reading: 'The Uzbeks' (Bennett & Bloom, 2003)

BASIC UZBEK GRAMMAR

Uzbek — or O'zbek — belongs to the Altaic family of languages, which takes its name from the Altai Mountains of Central Asia (according to recent research, the site of Genghis Khan's tomb). Other members of this family include Azerbaijani, Kazakh, Turkish, and, more distantly, Mongolian. After Turkish, Uzbek is the second largest of the group of related Turkic languages.

Until the 1920s, it was written in an Arabic-based script (which had also been used for its immediate ancestor Chagatai) and over the following decades there were various moves in the republic of Uzbekistan to convert the language to the Roman alphabet and then a modified Cyrillic version. With independence in the 1990s, a new Roman script is being gradually introduced (see page 20).

━Structure

While totally unrelated to English, the structure of Uzbek is nevertheless quite simple. In word order, the verb is usually put at the end of the sentence, e.g.

Men o'zbekcha bilaman.
'I speak Uzbek.' (literally: 'I Uzbek know.')

Uzbek is virtually free of grammatical irregularities, and this is helped by the fact that it is an 'agglutinative' language, meaning that it adds information at the end of the word in clear, distinct segments, e.g.

ish 'work'
ish-siz 'work-less' (= 'unemployed')
ish-siz-lik 'work-less-ness' (= 'unemployment')

yoz 'write'
yoz-ayap 'writing'
yoz-ayap-ti 'he/she/it is writing'
yoz-ayap-ti-lar 'they are writing'
yoz-ma-ayap-ti-lar 'they are not writing'

Although a trifle extreme, you can build up clearly understandable words like **tanishtirilmaganligidan** — 'because they were not introduced to each other.' Basically this breaks down as **tani** 'to get to know' + **(i)sh** 'together' + **tir** *causative* + **il** *passive* + **ma** 'not' + **gan** *past* + **lik** (=**lig-**) *abstract noun suffix* + **i** 'of' + **dan** 'from'/ 'due to'!

▬Nouns

Uzbek has no words for 'the,' 'a' or 'an' in the same way as English does — instead the meaning is generally undestood from the context, e.g. **kishi** can mean 'the person,' 'a person' or just simply 'person.'

Nouns form their plural by simply adding **-lar**, e.g. **mashina** 'car' → **mashinalar** 'cars,' **jurnal** 'magazine' → **jurnallar** 'magazines.'

The genitive form is **-ning**, e.g. **idoraning** 'office's' or 'of the office,' **kitobning** 'book's,' **kitoblarning** 'books'.' For more on genitive constructions, see the section on possessives.

Uzbek is a great language for active wordbuilding, and three important suffixes to note are:

-chi 'one who does, -er,' e.g. **ish** 'work' → **ishchi** 'worker,' **ov** 'hunting' → **ovchi** 'hunter'

-cha creates a language, e.g. **o'zbek** 'Uzbek' (person) → **o'zbekcha** 'Uzbek (language),' **Yaponiya** 'Japan' → **yaponcha** 'Japanese (language)'

-lik makes 'concept' nouns, e.g. **vazir** 'minister' → **vazirlik** 'ministry,' **issiq** 'hot' → **issiqlik** 'heat.'

—Adjectives

Adjectives are like nouns in that they can take the same endings. They always come before the noun, e.g.

'new' **yangi**	—	**yangi mashina**	'new car'
'old' **eski**	—	**eski mashina**	'old car'

Some other basic adjectives are:

open **ochiq**	quick **tez**
shut **yopiq**	slow **sekin**
cheap **arzon**	big **katta**
expensive **qimmat**	small **kichkina**
hot **issiq**	old *person* **qari**
cold **sovuq**	young **yosh**
near **yaqin**	good **yaxshi**
far **uzoq**	bad **yomon**

A common way of creating adjectives from other words is to add **-li** at the end of a word, e.g. **kuchli** 'strong' (**kuch** = 'strength'), **foydali** 'useful' (**foyda** = 'use'), etc. Adding **-siz** gives the meaning of 'without' or '-less,' e.g. **kuchsiz** 'weak,' **foydasiz** 'useless.'

—Adverbs

Most adverbs have a single form which never changes. Some examples:

here **bu yer(da)**	up **tepaga**
there **u yer(da)**	down **pastga**
well **yaxshi**	now **hozir**
badly **yomon**	tomorrow **ertaga**

Some are duplicated, like **qayta-qayta** 'repeatedly' (from **qayta** 'again') or **sekin-sekin** ('slowly', 'quietly'), while others have the same form as the corresponding adjective, e.g. **tez** means 'rapid' or 'rapidly.'

—Postpositions

Uzbek has postpositions — where words like 'in,' 'at' and 'behind' come *after* the noun and not before it as in

English (though remember that you can say 'who *with?*' as well as '*with* who?' — and there's no change in meaning). They sometimes modify the ending of the word and can be joined to that word:

to; for **-ga**	under **tagida**
at; in **-da**	after **-dan keyin**
from **-dan**	in front of **oldida**

e.g. **O'zbekistonda** 'in Uzbekistan,' **Angliyadan** 'from England.'

▬Pronouns

Personal pronouns can add on endings just like nouns. Basic forms are as follows:

SINGULAR	PLURAL
I **men**	we **biz**
you *singular* **siz**	you *plural* **sizlar**
he/she/it **u**	they **ular**

Possessive pronouns are:

SINGULAR	PLURAL
my **-(i)m**	our **-(i)miz**
your **-(i)ng**	your **-(i)ngiz**
his/her/its **-(s)i**	their **-lari**

e.g.   **jurnalim** 'my magazine'
       jurnali 'his/her/its magazine'
       jurnalimiz 'our magazine'

Postpositions add onto these endings, e.g. **maktab-im-dan** 'from my school' (literally: 'school-my-from').

   Possessive pronouns are also used to express a variety of possession and other relationships between words. Sometimes adding **-ning** (see page 11), sometimes not, this form gives us 'of,' e.g. **Fredning televizori** (literal-

---

* Another form of 'you' *singular* is **sen**, which corresponds to the English 'thou', it is used in highly informal situations and should be avoided by foreigners for fear of seeming impolite.

ly: 'Fred of television his') = 'Fred's television' (or 'the television of Fred'), **O'zbek tili** (literally; 'Uzbek language its') = 'Uzbek language'. This also gives us constructions like: **xalq muziqasi** 'folk music,' **idora ishchisi** 'office worker,' etc.

Use the dictionary section to work out what these genitive constructions mean:

rok kontserti   **kredit kartochkasi**
futbol matchi   **sputnik telefoni**
          radio programmasi

Demonstratives:

bu/shu this   **bular** these
u/o'sha that   **ular** those

▬Verbs

Verbs are very easy to form by adding a wide number of suffixes to the end of the basic verb form. While the structure of Uzbek verbs is very different from English, in fact it is extremely logical and clearly set out, although in practise it can sometimes be a little complex to extract the necessary information packed in at the end of each verb.

It is worth spending a little time sorting out the concept, and then you will meet with little difficulty in working out the distinct parts of an Uzbek sentence!

Every Uzbek verb has a basic form that carries a basic meaning. To the end of this are added smaller words or single vowels that provide further information to tell you who's doing what and how and when, e.g.

ber- 'give'
bermoq 'to give'
berdim 'I gave'
beraman 'I give/will give'
beryapman 'I am giving'

Other endings carry even more information, e.g.

berdir- 'cause to give'
berol- 'able to give'
bermoqchi- 'want to give'

We saw the personal pronouns above, but these are only used for emphasis. Like French or Spanish, the verb already gives this information, as the following endings for the past tense show:

SINGULAR	PLURAL
I **-dim**	we **-dik**
you *singular* **-dingiz**	you *plural* **-dinglar**
he/she/it **-di**	they **-lar**

e.g. **ko'rdim** I saw   **ko'rdik** we saw
ko'rdingiz you saw   **ko'rdinglar** you saw
ko'rdi he/she/it saw   **ko'rdilar** they saw

Uzbek, like the other Turkic languages, is amazingly regular, but it does have more than one way of expressing person in the verb, and this will vary from tense to tense. Another common set of person indicators is as follows:

ko'raman I see   **ko'ramiz** we see
ko'rasiz you see   **ko'rasizlar** you see
ko'radi he/she/it sees   **ko'radilar** they see

Mi is placed at the end of the sentence to reinforce when a question is being asked, e.g. **Avtobus bormi?** 'Is there a bus?', or with longer sentences such as **Siz inglizcha bilasizmi?** 'Do you speak English?'

Negatives vary in form according to tense. **Ma** 'not' is added to the verb itself, e.g. **berdim** 'I gave' — **bermadim** 'I did not give,' **to'xta!** 'stop!' — **to'xtamang!** 'don't stop!'

Emas is also used, but as a separate word, e.g. **Bu yaxshi emas.** 'This isn't good.'

▬Essential verbs

The verb 'to be' is expressed in a variety of ways. The most common form you will find is the simple series of present endings:

SINGULAR	PLURAL
-man I am	**-miz** we are
-san you are	**-siz** you are
-dir he/she/it is	**-dilar** they are

e.g. **Men tayyorman.** 'I am ready.' (literally: 'I ready am.')

The verb 'to have' is also expressed in a variety of ways. The most common forms you will encounter are **bor** 'there is/are' and **yo'q** 'there is/are not' — which are used with the possessive endings, e.g.

Mashinam bor. 'I have a car.'
(literally: 'My car there is.')
Vaqtim yo'q. 'I do not have time.'
(literally: 'My time there is not.')

▬A general note on language

Russian has had a great influence on the Uzbek spoken in the former Soviet Union, so many terms that are in common use are borrowed from Russian. In this guide we have tried to keep the language as "Uzbek" as possible yet still provide terms that are commonly used. For this reason, we have in some cases opted in favor of a Russian term where the Uzbek term is less common.

PRONUNCIATION GUIDE

Uzbek letter	Uzbek example	Approximate English equivalent
a	**apteka** 'pharmacy'	*a*pple
b	**bayram** 'holiday'	*b*ox
d	**do'kon** 'shop'	*d*og
e	**ellik** 'fifty'	p*e*t
f	**futbol** 'soccer'	*f*at
g	**gaz** 'gas'	*g*ot
h	**ha** 'yes'	*h*at
i	**ish** 'work'	h*i*t
j	**jaz** 'jazz'	*j*et
k	**kino** 'cinema'	*k*ick
l	**yulduz** 'star'	*l*et
m	**mashina** 'car'	*m*at
n	**neft** 'oil'	*n*et
o	**idora** 'office'	s*aw*
p	**prezident** 'president'	*p*et
q	**qizil** 'red'	(see note on page 18)
r	**radio** 'radio'	*r*at, but 'rolled' as in Spanish
s	**suv** 'water'	*s*it
t	**taksi** 'taxi'	*t*en
u	**muz** 'ice'	sh*oo*t
v	**vaqt** 'time'	*w*orld, *or v*an
x	**xabarlar** 'news'	lo*ch*, as in Scottish English
y	**yo'l** 'road'	*y*es
z	**zilzila** 'earthquake'	*z*ebra
o'	**so'z** 'word'	n*o*se
g'	**g'arb** 'west'	(see note on page 18)
sh	**shahar** 'town'	*sh*ut
ch	**choy** 'tea'	*ch*urch

ng	**ming** 'thousand'	si*ng*
'	**ma'no** 'meaning'	(see note below)

Nothing beats listening to a native speaker, but the following notes should help give you some idea of how to pronounce the following letters.

▬Vowels

1) Note that vowels are always pronounced separately of each other but with a smooth join of the sounds, e.g. **modafaa** ('defense') is pronounced '**modafa-a**,' **soat** ('hour'/'o'clock') is '**so-at**,' **tabiiy** ('natural') is '**tabi-iy**.'
2) The combination **uw** is sometimes pronounced as a long **u** (as in 'sh*oo*t'), e.g. **suv** 'water' is pronounced as '**suw**.'
3) The combination **iy** occurs at the ends of words and is pronounced as a long **i** (as in 'h*ea*t'), e.g. **tabiiy**, **ajnabiy** 'foreign.'

▬Consonants

g' is pronounced like a sort of growl in the back of your throat — like when you're gargling. Frequently transcribed into English for other languages that have this sound as 'gh', the German or Parisian 'r' is the easy European equivalent. [= Arabic غ]

x is the rasping 'ch' in Sottish 'loch' and German 'ach', frequently transcribed in English as 'kh'. It is also pronounced like the Spanish/Castillian 'jota'. [= Arabic/Persian خ]

q is pronounced like a **k**, but right back in your mouth at the throat end. Imagine you have a marble in the back of your throat and that you're bouncing it using only your glottis, and make a **k** sound at the same time. [= Persian or Arabic ق]

' is what is called the 'glottal stop'. In Uzbek, when it comes before a consonant, it prolongs the preceding vowel, sometimes with a slight 'creak' of breath separating the two, e.g. **ma'no** is pronounced '**maano**,' **a'lo** as '**aalo**,' **she'r** as '**she'er**.' When it comes after a consonant, it is usually pronounced as a sort of stop or catch in the flow of breath before articulating the following vowel, e.g. **san'at** is pronounced in two distinct segments as '**san-at**.' [= Turkish **'**/Persian ع]

▬Spelling notes

1) Like English, there are alternations of consonants in the spoken language which are not reflected in the spelling, particularly when final, most notably **b/p, b/v, f/v, p/f, z/s, n/m**, without change of meaning, e.g. **kitob** 'book' is pronounced '**kitop**,' **ozod** 'free' is '**ozot**,' **shanba** 'Saturday' is '**shamba**.' Unlike English, however, these are usually predictable, have no effect on meaning, and are easily picked up once you have found your 'Uzbek ear.' Note also that **d** and **t** are occasionally dropped at the ends of words in conversation, e.g. you might hear '**Samarqan**' for **Samarqand**, or '**do's**' for **do'st** ('friend').

2) Consonants can be 'doubled', e.g. **jurnallar** 'magazines' is pronounced very distinctly as '**jurnal-lar**,' **ikki** '2' as '**ik-ki**', **katta** 'big' as '**kat-ta**.' Doubled consonants are not pronounced in words which reflect foreign spelling, especially words of Russian origin, e.g. **programma** 'program,' **metall** 'metal,' and **kongress** 'congress'.

3) Remember that **h**, as a separate letter, is always pronounced in combinations like **mahsulot** ('**mah-sulot**') 'product,' **mashhur** ('**mash-hur**') 'famous'. It is often pronounced as a **x**, e.g. **raxmat!** for **rahmat!** 'thank you!'

The Uzbek Latín alphabet

Uzbek letter	Name of letter	Uzbek letter	Name of letter
A a	a	R r	re
B b	be	S s	se
D d	de	T t	te
E e	e	U u	u
F f	fe	V v	ve
G g	ge	X x	xe
H h	he	Y y	ye
I i	i	Z z	ze
J j	je	O' o'	o'
K k	ke	G' g'	g'e
L l	le	SH sh	she
M m	me	CH ch	che
N n	ne	NG ng	nge
O o	o	'	tutuq belgisi*
P p	pe		
Q q	qe		

The Uzbek Cyríllíc alphabet**

Uzbek letter	Roman equivalent	Name of letter	Uzbek letter	Roman equivalent	Name of letter
А а	[a]	a	Т т	[t]	te
Б б	[b]	be	У у	[u]	u
В в	[v]	ve	Ф ф	[f]	fe
Г г	[g]	ge	Х х	[x]	xe
Д д	[d]	de	Ц ц	[–]	tse
Е е	[e/ye]	e	Ч ч	[ch]	che
Ё ё	[yo]	yo	Ш ш	[sh]	she
Ж ж	[j]	je/zhe	Ъ ъ	[']	ayirish belgisi
З з	[z]	ze			
И и	[i]	i	Ь ь	[–]	yumshatish belgisi
Й й	[y]	qisqa i			
К к	[k]	ke	Э э	[e]	e
Л л	[l]	el	Ю ю	[u/yu]	yu
М м	[m]	em	Я я	[a/ya]	ya
Н н	[n]	en	Ў ў	[o]	o
О о	[o']	o	Қ қ	[q]	qe
П п	[p]	pe	Ғ ғ	[g']	g'e
Р р	[r]	er	Ҳ ҳ	[h]	he
С с	[s]	es			

* Also called 'apostrof'.
** A few letters or combinations occur only in Russian words.

UZBEK
Dictionary

UZBEK–ENGLISH
O'ZBEKCHA-INGLIZCHA

A

achchiq hot; spicy; bitter
adabiyot literature
adabsiz rude
adaptor adapter
adirlar foothills
Adliya Vazirligi Ministry of Justice
administrator administrator
admiral admiral
adolat justice
adres address
adres daftari directory
advokat lawyer
adyol blanket
aeroport airport
aeroport solig'i airport tax
afg'on Afghan
Afg'oniston Afghanistan
afsona legend
afsus unfortunate
afsuski unfortunately
agronom agronomist
ahamiyat importance
ahamiyatli important
ahmoq fool
aholi population
ahvol state; condition
ajdod ancestor
ajnabiy foreign
ajoyib surprising
aka older brother
akademik academic
akademiya academy
akilla- to bark
akkumulyator battery *car*
aksent accent

aktivist activist
albatta certainly; of course
alda- to fool
alifbo alphabet
allergiya allergy; ...-ga allergi-yam bor I'm allergic to . . .
almashtir- to replace; to exchange
alo! hello!
alomat symptom; sign
aloqa connection; relationship
aloqalar communications
alpinistlar boltasi ice ax
amaki paternal uncle
Amerika America
Amerika Qo'shma Shtatlari (AQSh) U.S.A.
amerikalik American
ammo however
amortizator bumper
amputatsiya amputation
ana u that *preposition*
an'anaviy traditional
anchadan beri for a long time
anekdot joke
anesteziolog anesthetist
angar hangar
Angliya England
aniq certain; exact
anor pomegranate
antibiotik antibiotic
antifriz anti-freeze
antiseptik antiseptic
apelsin orange *fruit*
apenditsit appendicitis
apparat machine
aprel April
apteka pharmacy
aqldan ozgan insane

AQSh (Amerika Qo'shma Shtatlari) U.S.A.
arab Arab
arabcha Arabic language
aralashmalardan tozala- to refine
aralashmalardan tozalovchi zavod refinery
aravacha cart
archa bayrami New Year; Christmas
arg'imchoq swing
ari bee; wasp
ariq ditch
arman Armenian
Armaniston Armenia
armiya army
aroq vodka; liquor
aroqxo'r alcoholic
aroqxo'rlik alcoholism
arpa barley
arqon rope
arra saw
artillerya artillery
artist actor; performer
arxeologik archaeological
arxeologika archaeology
arxitekt architect
arxitektura architecture
arzon cheap
arzonroq cheaper
asab nerve
asal honey
asal oyi honeymoon
asar composition
asboblar tools
asbob-uskunalar equipment
ashula song
ashula ayt- to sing
asir prisoner; P.O.W.; hostage
asirlar lageri P.O.W. camp
askar soldier
asl origin
asliy original
asos base; basis
asosiy main

aspirin aspirin
asr century
assalomu alaykum! hello!; *to which the reply is* **alaykum assalom** *(formal) or just* **assalomu alaykum**
astma asthma
astmali asthmatic
atir perfume
atirgul rose
atlas atlas
atlas ko'ylak Uzbek silk dress
atletika athletics
atrof area
avariya accident; crash; emergency
avariya holatida chiqish emergency exit
avgust August
aviaxat air mail
avliyo saint
Avstraliya Australia
avstraliyalik Australian
avtobus bus
avtomat machine gun
avtonom autonomous
avtonomiya autonomy
avtor author
avtostantsiya bus station
axborot agenti news agency
axborot news
axborot vositalari media
axlat garbage; rubbish
aybla- accuse
ayg'ir stallion
ayiq bear
aylan- to spin; to walk around
ayniqsa especially
ayol woman; female
ayollar sartaroshxonasi beauty parlor
ayollar sartaroshxonasi hairdresser
ayt- to say; to tell; to express
aziz dear; loved
a'zo member

B

bachadon womb
bachkana silly; childish
badan body
badan tarbiya exercise
bagaj baggage
bagaj joyi trunk of car
bagaj kamerasi baggage counter
bahona excuse
bahor spring season
bajar- to perform *duty*
bak tank
bakteriya bacteria
baland high; loud
baland bo'yli tall
balandlik kasalligi altitude sickness
baland ovoz bilan loudly
balet ballet
baliq fish
baliq ovlash fishing
Balkar Balkar
balki maybe; perhaps
balkon balcony
ballon inner-tube
Ballon teshilgan. I have a flat tire/puncture.
Band. The line is busy.
bandit bandit
bank bank
banka can/tin; canister
banka ochadigan can opener
bankir banker
banknot bank note
baqir- to shout
bar bar
barak barracks
barg leaf
barmen bartender
barmoq finger
barrel barrel *of oil*
basketbol basketball
basseyn swimming pool

bastakor composer
batareya battery
bayram holiday
baytal mare
ba'zan sometimes
ba'zi some
beg'araz humanitarian
beg'araz yordam humanitarian aid
beg'araz yordam ko'rsatuvchi aid worker
beg'araz yordam tashkiloti charity *organization*
begona stranger
begunoh innocent
behazil no joke; seriously
bekat bus stop
bekitib qo'y- to hide
bekor qil- to cancel
bel back *noun*
bel og'rig'i backache
belgi mark; sign; symbol; symptom
belkurak shovel
benzin petrol; gas
bepul free of charge
ber- to give
besh five
bet face; cheek; page
beva widow; widower
Bevaman. I am widowed.
bevosita direct
bifshteks steak
bil- to know *something*; **Bilaman.** I know.; **Bilmadim.** I don't know.
bilaguzuk bracelet
bilak wrist
bilan and; with
bilan birga along with
bilet ticket
bilim knowledge
bino building
bir one; a; **bir kishilik xona** a single room
bir amallab somehow
bir joyda somewhere

bir marta once
bir narsa something
bir necha several; some
bir nima something
bir tomonlama yo'l one-way street
bir varaq qog'oz a piece of paper
bir-biri each other
birdan suddenly
birga together
birinchi first
birinchi klass/sinf first class
birlash- to unite
birlashgan united
Birlashgan Millatlar Maorif, Ilm, va Madaniyat Tashkiloti UNESCO
Birlashgan Millatlar Qochoqlar uchun Oliy Komissari UNHCR
Birlashgan Millatlar Taraqqiyot Programmasi UNDP
Birlashgan Millatlar Tashkiloti United Nations
birlashish unification
bit louse/lice
bitir- to end; to finish
bitta single; **bitta (buxonka non)** loaf; **bitta pivo** a bottle of beer
bittasi someone/somebody
biz we
biznes klas business class
biznesmen businessman/woman
bizniki ours
bizning our
blyuz blues *music*
bob chapter
bodring cucumber
bog' park
bog'cha garden; yard
bog'ich sling *medical*
bo'g'il- to choke
Bo'g'ilyapti. He is choking.
bog'la- to tie

boj customs duty
bojxona customs *border*
boks boxing
bo'l- to be; to become; to happen; to divide
bola child
bo'ladiganga o'xshaydi likely
bolalar children
bo'ldi! that's enough!
bolg'a hammer
bo'lim section
bo'lish- to share
bolnitsa hospital
bo'lsa ham although
Bo'lsa kerak. Iit is probable.
bolta ax
bomba bomb
bombardimon bombardment
bombardirovkachi bomber
bomba zararsizlantirish bomb disposal
boq- to care
... bor there is/are; have
bor- to go; **...-ga bor-** to visit *a place*; **mehmonga/uyiga bor-** to visit *a person*
bo'ri wolf
borish bileti one-way ticket
borish-kelish bileti return ticket
bo'ron storm
Borsak kerak. We'll probably go.
bos- to print; to raid
bosh head; chief; boss; leader; main; beginning; **Boshim og'riyapti.** I have a headache.
bo'sh empty; barren
bosh aylantir- to confuse; **Boshim aylanyapti.** I feel dizzy.
bosh barmoq thumb
bo'sh qolgan dala fallowland
bo'sh vaqt free time
bosh vazir prime minister
bo'shat- to empty

boshga ol- to reverse
boshla- to lead; to guide; to begin
boshliq head; chief; boss; leader
bo'shmi: Bu joy bo'shmi? Is this seat free?
boshqa different; other
boshqalar rest; others
boshqar- to control
boshqasiga jo'nat- to forward
bosim pressure
bosqin invasion
bot- to sink
botqoq marsh; swamp
boy rich
bo'y coast
bo'ya- to paint
Bo'ydoqman. I am single. *said by a man*
bo'yin neck
boyo'g'li owl
bo'yoq paint
bozor market; **bozor qil-** to go shopping
bozor kuni Sunday
Britaniya Britain
britaniyalik British
britva razor
bron reservation; **Joy bronlasam bo'ladimi?** Can I reserve a place?; **Joyni bronlaganman.** I have a reservation.
bronemashina armored car
bronla- to reserve
bronlangan reserved
broshka brooch
bu this; **bu hafta** this week; **bu taraf** this way; **bu yil** this year
buddist Buddhist
buddo dini Buddhism
bug'doy wheat
bugun today; **bugun ertalab** this morning; **bugun kechasi** tonight; **bugun obeddan keyin** this afternoon

bular these
bulg'arskiy sweet pepper
buloq spring *of water*
bulut cloud
bumajnik wallet
buqa bull
burchak angle; corner
burga flea
burgut eagle
buril- turn
burilish bend in road
burun nose
buterbrot sandwich
butun entire; whole
buva grandfather
buvi grandmother
buxgalter accountant
buyrak kidney
buyruq order
buyuk great
buyur- to order *someone*
buz- to spoil
buzoq calf *cow*
byudjet budget

CH

chal- to play *a musical instrument*
chalg'i o'roq scythe
chamadon suitcase
chang'i uchadigan joy ski slope
chang'i uchish skiing
chang'i yo'li ski piste
Chanqab ketdim. I'm thirsty.
chap left; **chapga buriling!** turn left!
chaq- to sting
chaqir- to call; to invite
chaqmoq lighter
chaqmoq tosh flint
charcha- to tire
charchagan tired
chashka cup
chayna- to chew

chayqat- to shake
chechen Chechen
Chechnya Chechnya
chegara border; frontier
chegarachi border guard
chegara punkti border crossing
chek check *of money*
chek- to smoke
chekin- to withdraw
chekish smoking; **chekish mumkin emas** no smoking
chelak bucket
cherkez Circassian
chet limit
chet ellik foreigner
chida- to last
chin real
chinor plane tree
chipqon boil
chiq- to go out
chiqar- to expel
chiqib ket- to leave
chiqish exit
chirkov church
chiroq light; lamp
chiroqlar lighting
chiroyli beautiful
chislo date
chisnok garlic
chivin mosquito
chiz- to draw
chiziq line
cho'chqa pig
cho'chqa g'oshti pork
chodir tent
chodir qurish camping
chodir tikiladigan joy campsite
cho'kka tush- to kneel
cho'l desert
cho'mil- to bathe
cho'ntak pocket
chop- to run; to chop
cho'p stick
chopon Uzbek coat
cho'pon shepherd
cho'pon iti sheepdog
cho'qqi peak; summit

chorshanba Wednesday
cho'tka brush
choy tea; breakfast
choygun kettle
choy qoshig'i teaspoon
choyshab sheet
cho'z- to extend; to lengthen
chuchvara wonton
chumoli ant
chunki because
chuqur deep
chuvalchang earthworm

D

-da on
dada father
daftar notebook
dahshatli terrible
dala field; plain *noun*
dam ol- to rest; to relax
dam olish rest; **dam olish uchun tanaffus** break for refreshments
dam olish payti vacation
-dan because of; through; **-dan katta** bigger than; **-dan kichkina** smaller than; **-dan tufayli** for that reason
-dan beri since
-dan boshqa except (for) . . .
-dan keyin after
-dan ko'p/ko'proq more
-dan oldin before
dangasa lazy
daniyalik Danish
daraxt tree
daraxtzor wood; forest; copse
dars lesson
darvoza gate
daryo river
daryocha stream
darz fracture
darz ket- to fracture
dastak handle

dastlabki original
dasturxon tablecloth
davlat nation; state
davlat boshlig'i head of state
davlat to'ntarilishi coup d'etat
davo cure
davola- to cure; to treat
davom et- continue
davomida during
davr era; reign
dazmol iron *for clothes*
de- to say; to mean
defitsit shortage
dehqon farmer
dehqonchilik farming; agriculture
dekabr December
demokratik democratic
demokratiya democracy
dengiz sea
dengiz floti navy
deraza window
desert dessert
devor wall
deyarli almost
dezodorant deodorant
diagnoz diagnosis
dieta diet
digital digital
diktator dictator
diktatorlik dictatorship
din religion
dinamo dynamo
diplomatik aloqalar diplomatic
   ties
direktor manager
disk jokey disk jockey
diskoteka disco
dizel diesel
dod! help!
Dog'iston Daghestan
dog'istonlik Daghestani
doira circle
do'kon store; shop
do'kondor shopkeeper
doktor doctor
dokument document;
   Dokumentingiz bormi? Do

you have any I.D.?
do'l sleet
dollar dollar
dom apartment block/complex
domkrat jack car
dori drug; medicine; medication;
   fertilizer
dovon mountain pass; crossing
do'zax hell
dunyo world
duo qil- to pray
dur pearl
duradgor carpenter
durbin binoculars; telescope
dush shower
dushanba Monday
dushman enemy
duxovkada pishir- to bake

echki goat
egil- to lean
egizak twins
ehtimol probable
ehtiyot careful
ehtiyotlik care
ek- to sow
ekin ek- to grow crops
ekinlar crops
ekish planting
ekonomika economics
ekonomist economist
eksport export
eksport qil- to export
ekspress express; fast
elchi ambassador; diplomat
elchixona embassy
elektr electricity
elektron buyumlar do'koni
   electrical goods store
elektron pochta e-mail
elektron pochta adresi e-mail
   address
ellik fifty

emal enamel
eman oak
emas not
Emlanganman. I have been vaccinated.
enaga midwife
eng -est; **eng buyuk** greatest; **eng katta** biggest; **eng yaxshi** best
eng kamida at least
epchil skilled
epidemiya epidemic
epilepsiya epilepsy
episkop bishop
er husband
eri- to dissolve; to thaw
erkak male
erkak kishi man
Eron Iran
eronlik Iranian
ertaga tomorrow
ertalab morning; a.m.
er-xotinlik marriage
esdan chiqar- to forget
eshak donkey
eshik door
eshit- to hear; to listen
eskalator escalator
eski old *things*
Eski Shahar Old City
esla- to remember
etaj floor; story
etik boot
etnik tozalash ethnic cleansing

F

fabrika factory
faks fax
faks apparati fax machine
fakt fact
familiya surname
fanlar akademiyasi academy of sciences
faol activist
faqat only
faqatgina just
farqli different
fasl season
fayl computer file
federatsiya federation
fe'l verb
fen hairdryer
ferma farm
fermer farmer
fevral February
fikr idea; thought
filtrlangan filtered
filtrsiz filterless
firma business; firm
fizika physics
fizioterapiya physiotherapy
fizkultura exercise
folklor folklore
fonetika phonetics
forma uniform
fors Persian *person*
forsi Farsi
forum forum
fotoapparat camera
fotoapparat jihozlari camera equipment
fotograf photographer
fotografiya photography
fotokopiya photocopy
foyda worth
foydalan- to use; to take advantage of
foydali useful
frantsuz French
frantsuzcha French language
funt pound
fuqaro citizen; civilian
fuqaro huquqlari civil rights
fuqarolar urushi civil war
fuqarolik citizenship
furgon van
fursat occasion
futbol soccer
futbol matchi soccer match

G

-ga to; for
-gacha until
GAI traffic police
gala flock of birds
g'alaba victory
g'alati strange
g'alla grain
galon gallon
galstuk tie; necktie
gamburger hamburger
gangrena gangrene
gap speech; talk; issue; **Gapingiz to'g'ri.** You are right.; **Gapingiz noto'g'ri.** You're wrong.; **Nima gaplar?** What's up?
gapir- to talk; to speak
garaj garage
g'aram haystack
g'arb west *noun*
g'arbiy west; western
garmdori red
garnizon garrison
gavan harbour
g'avvos diver
gayka klyuchi spanner; wrench
gaz gas
gaz baloni gas bottle; butane canister
gaz ishlab chiqarish gas production
gaz maydoni gas field
gaz pedali accelerator
gaz qudug'i gas well
gazeta newspaper
gazli sparkling drink
gazli suv mineral water
general general *noun*
general shtab headquarters
genotsid genocide
geolog geologist
Germaniya Germany
gid guide
gigant giant
gigiena hygiene
gilam carpet; rug
g'ildirak wheel
ginekolog gynecologist
gipertoniya low blood pressure
gipotoniya high blood pressure
g'isht brick
giyohvand drug addict
go'dak baby; infant
gol goal *football*
golf golf
gollandiyalik Dutch
g'or cave
gorchitsa mustard
gorispolkom city hall; town hall
go'sht meat
g'oz goose
go'zallik beauty
gramm gram
grammatika grammar
granata grenade
grek Greek
grek tili Greek language
gripp flu/influenza
gruppa group
gruzin Georgian
gruzincha Georgian language
Gruziya Georgia
gruzovoy mashina truck
gubka sponge
gugurt matches; **Gugurtingiz bormi?** Do you have a light?
gul flower
gulfurush florist
gumbaz dome
gumburlash thunder
guruch (uncooked) rice
g'urur pride
guvoh witness

H

ha yes
hafta week

hakam

hakam referee; judge
hali yet
hali ham still *adverb*
hal qil- to solve
ham and; also
ham ..., ham ... both ... and
hamkasb colleague
hamkorlik co-operation
hamma all; everybody/every-one
hamma birga all together
hamma narsa everything
hammom bathroom; Turkish baths
hamshira nurse
haq compensation; pay; payment
...haqida about
haqiqat truth; reality
haqiqiy real; actual
har (bir) every; har bitta each; har doim always; har kuni every day; har xil all kinds; har xillik variety
harakat qil- to try; to make an effort
harbiy military
harbiy havo kuchlari air force
hashorat insect
hashorat tushiradigan dori insecticide
havo air; weather; Havo bulut. It's cloudy; Havo sovuq. It is cold.
havo yo'llari airline
hayda- to drive
haykal statue
hayot life
hayvon animal
hayvonot bog'i zoo
hazil joke
hazillash- to joke
hech kim no one; nobody
hech nima nothing
hech qachon never
hech qayer nowhere

Hechqisi yo'q. It doesn't matter.; No problem!
hid smell
hikmat wisdom
hikoya story; tale
himoya protection
himoya qil- to protect
hind Indian
hindu Hindu
hindu dini Hinduism
Hinduston India
his feeling
Hisob necha bo'ldi? What's the score/bill?
hojatxona bathroom
hoji pilgrim *to Mecca*
hokim ruler *person*
hol condition
ho'l wet
homilador pregnant; Homila-dorman. I'm pregnant.
homiladorlikdan saqlanish birth control
hosil harvest
hosila derivative *noun*
hovli garden; yard; courtyard
hozir now
hozirgi present *adjective*
hozirgi zamon present *time*
hujjat document; record; form
hujjatli film documentary film
hujum attack
hujum qil- to attack
hukmronlik reign
hukumat government
hunarmand craftsman
huquqlar rights
hurriyat freedom

ibodatxona temple
ich- to drink
ichiga into

ichiga kirmaydi excluded
ichiga ol- to contain
ichimlik drink
ichkari interior
ichki interior
ichki Ishlar Vazirligi Ministry of Internal Affairs
ichki reys national flight
idora office
iflos dirty
ifloslanish pollution
igna needle; pin
ijaraga ol- to hire
ijod qil- to create
ijtimoiy social
ikki two; **ikki kishilik karavot** double bed; **ikki kishilik xona** double room
ikki hafta fortnight
ikki marta twice
ikki yildan keyin the year after next
ikkinchi second *adjective*
ikkinchi klas second class
ikkovi both
ikra caviar
ilgari forwards
iliq warm
ilm science
ilmiy scientific
ilon snake
ilon chaqishi snake bite
iltimos! please!
immigrant immigrant
immigratsiya immigration
imo-ishora tili sign language
imom imam
import qil- to import
imtihon exam; test
imzo signature
indikator chirog'i indicator light
indinga the day after tomorrow
induk turkey
infarkt heart attack
ingichka thin *thing*
ingliz English

inglizcha English language
ingush Ingush
injener engineer
injil Bible
inqilob revolution
inson human
inson huquqlari human rights
insonparvarlik yordami humanitarian aid
institut institute; college
internet internet
interv'yu interview
ip string; thread
ipak silk
iqlim climate
iqtisod economics; economy
iqtisodchi economist
irlandiya Ireland
irlandiyalik Irish
isbot evidence; proof
isbotla- to prove
ish work; job
ishchi worker
ishg'ol occupation *of a country*
ishg'ol qiluvchilar/bosqinchilar occupying forces
ishla- to work
ishlat- to use
ishlatilgan second-hand
ishon- to believe
ishonma- to doubt
ishsiz unemployed
ishsizlik unemployment
ishtirok et- to participate
ishton underwear
isitma fever; **Isitmam bor.** I have a temperature.
Islom Islam
ism name; noun; **Ismingiz nima?** What is your name?; **Ismim Fred.** My name is Fred.
ispancha Spanish language
ispaniyalik Spanish person
Isroil Israel
issiq warm; hot; **issiq suv** hot water

issiqlik heat
ista- to desire; to wish
isyonchi rebel
it dog
italiyan Italian person
Italya Italy
italyancha Italian language
itar- to push
ittifoq union
ixtiro (qilingan narsa) invention
ixtirochi inventor
iyak chin
iyul July
iyun June
izla- to look for; to seek; to search for

J

jadval timetable
jag' jaw
jahli chiqqan angry
jallod executioner
jamiyat society
jamoat community
jang battle
jangchi fighter
janjal fight
jannat heaven; paradise
janoza funeral
janub south *noun*
janubiy south; southern
jarima fine *of money*; reparation
jarroh surgeon
javob answer; explanation
javob ber- to reply
jaz jazz
jazola- to punish
jemper sweater
jeton token *coin*
jiddiy serious; grave
jigar liver
jigarrang brown
jihozlar equipment

jimjit silent
jimjitlik silence
jinni crazy; insane
jinoyat crime
jinoyatchi criminal
jins sex *anatomical*
jinsi shim jeans
jinsiy aloqa sexual relations
jinsiy a'zolar genitals
jo'mrak tap; faucet
jon soul; **Jonimga tegdi.** I am annoyed
joy place; location; position; seat
joynamoz prayer rug
juda too; very; **juda issiq payt** heatwave; **juda kam** too little; **juda ko'p** too many/much; **juda yaxshi/a'lo** excellent
jugut Jew
juma Friday
jumhuriyat republic
jun wool
jur'atli brave
jurnal magazine

K

kabel cable
kabob kebab
kaklik partridge
kalamush rat
kalit key
kalkulyator calculator
kalta short
kaltak stick
kaltakesak lizard
kamalak rainbow
kamar belt
kambag'al poor
kamchilik ovoz minority vote
kamroq less
kana tick *insect*
Kanada Canada
kanadalik Canadian
kanal canal; channel

kanikul vacation
kantselyariya do'koni stationer's
kantselyariya jihozlari stationery
kapalak butterfly
kapital capital *financial*
kapot bonnet/hood *of car*
kaptar pigeon
kar deaf
karam cabbage
karavot bed
karnay speaker *hi-fi*
karobka box
karta map
kartoshka potato
kartoteka file *paper*
karvon caravan
kasaba uyushmasi trade union
kasal sick; patient *medical*; Kasalman. I am sick.
kasallik illness; disease
kasalxona hospital
kasb occupation; job; profession
kashf et- discover
kashnich coriander
Kaspiy dengizi Caspian Sea
kassa cashier's booth; ticket office
kasseta cassette; tape
kassir cashier
katolik Catholic
katta big; senior
katta bo'l- to grow up
katta chuqurlikdagi platfo'rma deep-water platform
katta magazin department store
katta sumka carrier bag
kattalik size
kattaroq larger
kauchuk rubber
Kavkaz Caucasus
kayf pleasure
kazino casino
kech late; **kech qol-** to be late
kecha night; yesterday
kechiktir- delay
kechirasiz! excuse me!; sorry!

kechki payt evening
kechqurun evening
kechuv crossing
kel- to come; to arrive; to appear; **keling!** come in!
kelajak future
kelib chiqish origin
kelish jadvali arrivals
kelish muddati date of arrival
kema ship
keng thick; wide
kengash board; council
kerak need; it's necessary; **Sizga nima kerak?** What do you want?; **Menga . . . kerak.** I want . . .; **Menga . . . kerak emas.** I don't want . . .
keramika ceramics
kes- to cut
ket- to leave; **ketdik!** let's go!
ketchup ketchup
ketish jadvali departures
ketish muddati date of departure
keyin then
keyingi next
keyingi hafta next week
keyingi yil next year
keyinroq afterwards
kichik little
kichkina little; small
kichkinaroq smaller
kilo kilogram
kilometr kilometer
kim? who?
kim bo'lsa ham anyone; whoever
kino film/movie
kino(teatr) cinema
kiosk kiosk; newsstand
kipyatilnik heating coil
kir dirty; laundry
kir- to enter; **Kiring!** come in!
kir yuvish poroshogi detergent
kir yuvish xizmati laundry service
kirish entrance

kirish- undertake
kirish mumkin emas no entry
kishi person
kislorod oxygen
kitob book
kitob do'koni bookshop
kiy- to wear
kiyik deer
kiyim clothes
kiyim-kechak magazini clothes shop
kiyin- to get dressed; to put on *clothes*
klassik muzika classical music
klub club; nightclub
ko'ch- to move house
ko'cha street
ko'chadagi outside; Ko'chaga chiqdi. He went outside.
ko'chir- to copy
kod code; dialing code
kofe coffee
ko'k blue; green
ko'kartir- to bruise
ko'k choy green tea
ko'krak breast; chest
ko'k sulton sour plum
ko'l lake
kolgotka tights
kolledj college
kolxoz collective farm; kolkhoz
ko'm- to bury
kombayn combine harvester
kombinatsiya slip *clothing*
ko'mir coal
ko'mir koni coal mine
komissiya commission
kommanda team
kommunist communist
kommunizm communism
kompas compass
kompozitor composer
kompozitsiya composition
kompyuter computer
kon mine *mineral*

konchi miner
konditsionir air conditioner
konditsionir sistemasi air conditioning
konferentsiya conference
konferentsiya zali conference room
konfet candy
konki uchish skating
konkurs competition
konstitutsiya constitution
konsul'tant consultant
konsulxona consulate
kontakt linza contact lenses
kontakt linza saqlanadigan suyuqlik contact lens solution
konteyner container *freight*
kontrabandist smuggler
kontrakt contract
kontsert concert
kontsert zali concert hall
kontslager concentration camp
kontuziya concussion *medical*
konvert envelope
konvoy convoy
konyak cognac; brandy
ko'p many; a lot; much; most; often
ko'pay(tir)- to breed
ko'pchilik majority
ko'plik amount
ko'prik bridge
koptok ball
ko'r blind
ko'r- to see
ko'rfaz bay; gulf
ko'rgazma show; exhibition
ko'rpa(cha) quilt
korruptsiya corruption
ko'rsat- to show; to exhibit
kosa bowl
kostyum jacket
kostyum-shim suit
ko'tar- to lift; to raise
ko'tarib yuradigan televizor portable TV

ko'taril- to rise
kotib secretary
ko'ylak dress; shirt
ko'z eye
ko'z (ko'rish qobiliyati) eyesight
ko'zoynak (eye)glasses
kran crane *machine*; tap/faucet
kredit credit
kredit kartochkasi credit card
krizis crisis
kseroks photocopy
kseroks mashinasi photocopier
kseroks qil- to copy
kuch strength
kuchli strong
kuchsiz weak
kuchuk dog; puppy
kul- to laugh
kuldon ashtray
kulgili funny; humorous
kumush silver
kun day; date
kunbotar vaqti sunset
kun chiqish payti sunrise
kunduz daytime
kurak spade
kurash wrestling
kurash- to struggle
kurd Kurd
kur'er courier
kurort spa
Kurs qancha? What is the exchange rate?
kut- to wait (for); to expect
kutilmagan unexpected
kutubxona library
kuxnya kitchen
kuz autumn/fall
kuzatuvchi observer
kvartal quarter; area; housing estate/project
kvartira apartment
kvitantsiya receipt

lab lip
laboratoriya laboratory
lahza moment
lak varnish
lampochka light bulb
laptop kompyuter laptop computer
lat injury
latcha weasel
lat ye- to injure
lavlagi beetroot
laylak stork
lekin but
lektsiya lecture
leykoplastir Band-Aid
lezvie razorblade
lift lift; elevator
limetta lime
limon lemon
lineyka measure
linza lens
litr liter
lo'li Central Asian Gypsy
loviya beans
loy mud
lug'at dictionary

-ma not
machit mosque
madaniyat culture
madaniy hol marital status
madrasa madrasa
mafia mafia
mafioza gangster
magazin store
magnitli magnetic
magnitofon tape recorder
mag'rur proud
mahalla community
mahalliy local

mahrum qil-

mahrum qil- to deprive
mahsi soleless leather boots
mahsulot product
majburiyat obligation
majlis meeting; assembly
makaron pasta
makka jo'xori corn/maize
maktab school
ma'lum known
ma'lumot information
ma'lumotlar byurosi information office
ma'lumotnoma guidebook
mamlakat country
mamnun satisfied
man et- to forbid
man etilgan forbidden; illegal
mana ... here is/are . . .
mana bu this
manba source
ma'no meaning
manzara view
maorif education
maqbara mausoleum; tomb
maqola article; paper; report
maqsad goal; aim
maqta- to praise
marhamat! welcome!
marka stamp *postal*
markaz center
marshrut route
mart March
masal proverb
masala problem
mashhur famous; well-known
mashina car; machine
mashina dokumentlari/ hujjatlari car papers
mashinalarga qarshi mina anti-vehicle mine
mashina registratsiyasi car registration
mashina to'xtash joyi car park; parking lot
mashinka typewriter
mast drunk
masxaraboz clown

matbuot the press
match game; match
matematika mathematics
material material
mato material
matras mattress
mavzu subject
maxfiy secret *adjective*
maxorka qog'ozi cigarette papers
may May
mayda small; fine
mayda millat minority ethnic group
mayda pul loose change
maydon main square
Mazam yo'q. I am ill.
mazasiz tasteless
mebel' furniture
mehmon guest; visitor
mehmon notiq guest speaker
mehmonxona hotel; hostel; guesthouse
me'mor architect
men I
menejer manager
mening my
menyu menu
metal metal
metr meter
metro underground; subway; metro
meva fruit
meva suvi fruit juice
mexanik mechanic
mikroblar germs
mikroskop microscope
mil mile
militsioner policeman
militsiya police
militsiya uchastkasi police station
millat nation; people; nationality
million million
milliy traditional
milliy qirg'in ethnic cleansing
miltiq gun; rifle

min- to ride a horse
mina mine *explosive*
mina bos- to hit a mine
mina detektori mine detector
mina joylashtir- to lay mines
minalarni zararsizlantirish mine disposal
minalashtirilgan joy minefield
mina zararsizlantir- to clear mines
minbar podium
mineral mineral
ming thousand
Minnatdorman. I am grateful.
minora tower; minaret
mintaqa region
minut minute *of time*
mis copper
misol example
mix nail
moda fashion clothes
model model
modem modem
mohir skilled
mohirlik skill
mo'jiza miracle
mol cattle
mol go'shti beef
moliya finance
mo'ri chimney
morojniy ice cream
mos suitable
motor engine
mototsikl motorbike
mo'ylov mustache
muallif author
muddat period
Mudofaa Vazirligi Ministry of Defense
muhabbat love
muharrir editor
muhim important
muhojir immigrant
muhojirlik immigration
muhokama trial *legal*

mukofot prize
mullo mullah
mulohaza discussion
mulohaza qil- to discuss
muloyim kind *adjective*
mumkin maybe; possible; Mumkinmi? may I?
mumkin bo'lsa if possible
mumkin emas illegal; not possible
munchoq necklace
muqaddima introduction
mushuk cat
musicha dove
muslim Muslim
musobaqa contest
musor garbage
mustaqil independent
mustaqil davlat independent state
mustaqillik independence
mutaxassis specialist
muvaffaqiyat success
muvaffaqiyatsizlik failure
muxbir journalist
muxtor autonomous
muxtorlik autonomy
muz ice
muzday cool
muzey museum
muzika music
muzla- to freeze
muzokara olib boruvchi negotiator
muz qaymoq ice cream

na ... na ... emas. neither . . . nor
nafas breath
namoyish demonstration *political*
namoyish qil- to protest
namoyishchilar demonstrators *political*

namoz o'qi- to pray *Islamic*
narkoman drug addict
narkotik narcotic
narsa thing
narvon ladder
narx cost; price
nashr qil- to publish
nashriyot publisher
nasos pump
nasos bilan tort- to pump
nasos stantsiyasi pumping station
navbatchi guard
Navruz Persian New Year *March 21*
nazariya theory
nechta? how many?
neft oil; petroleum
neftchi oil worker
neft ishlab-chiqarish oil production
neft kamari oil pipeline
neft maydoni oilfield
neft qudug'i oil well
neft tankeri oil tanker
neft to'kilishi oil spill
nega? why?
nemis German
nemischa German language
nevara grandchild
neytral neutral drive/gear
nima? what?; **Nima u?** what's that?; **Nima bo'ldi?** What's the trouble?
niyat intention
nogiron disabled
nogironlar aravachasi wheelchair
nog'ora drum
nok pear
noma'lum unknown
nomer number
nomusga teg- to rape
non bread
nordon sour
noski sock(s)
nosvoy chewing tobacco

notiq speaker *of parliament*
noto'g'ri false; wrong
noto'g'ri tushun- to misunderstand
novvot rock sugar
novvoyxona bakery
noyabr November
nul nought; zero
nuqsonsiz perfect

O/O'

obed noon; lunch
obeddan keyin afternoon
obed qil- to lunch
ob qo'y- to keep
och rang light *not dark*
och- to open
ocherk article; paper; essay
ochiq open
o'chir- to switch off
ochki eyeglasses
odam person
odamlar people
odam o'g'risi kidnapper
odatda usually
oddiy normal; ordinary; usual
odob etiquette
odobli polite
ofat crisis; disaster
ofitsant waiter
ofitsantka waitress
ofitser officer military
oftob sunshine
og'il barn
o'g'il son
o'g'il bola boy
og'ir heavy
o'g'irla- to steal; to kidnap; ...-imni o'g'irlatdim. My ... has been stolen.
o'g'irlangan stolen
o'g'irlash robbery
og'irlik weight
o'g'it fertilizer

o'rnashtir-

og'iz mouth
og'iz chayish uchun suv
  mouthwash
o'g'ri thief; bandit
o'g'rilik theft
og'riq pain
og'riq qoldiruvchi anesthetic
og'riq qoldiruvchi dori
  painkiller
ohak lime
oila family
oktyabr October
ol- to take; to get; to receive; ...
  olaman. I'd like to order . . .
o'l- to die
o'lcha- to measure
old front *noun*
oldida in front of
oldin previously
oldingi forward *adjective*
oldingi kun the day before yesterday
o'ldir- to kill; to murder
o'ldirish execution
old oyna windscreen; windshield
o'lgan dead
olib kel- to bring
olib yur- to carry
olim scientist
o'lim death
o'lim jazosi execution
o'lim jazosiga hukm qil- to
  execute
Oliy Majlis Uzbek parliament
Ollo God
olma apple
olov fire
olti six
oltin gold
oltinchi sixth
oltmish sixty
olxo'ri plum
ombor depot; warehouse
o'n ten
ona mother
o'n besh fifteen

o'n bir eleven
o'ngga buriling! turn right!
o'ngchilar right-wingers
o'ng tomon right side
o'n ikki twelve
o'ninchi tenth
o'n olti sixteen
o'n sakkiz eighteen
o'n to'qqiz nineteen
o'n to'rt fourteen
o'n uch thirteen
o'n yetti seventeen
o'n yil decade
o'p- to kiss
opa older sister
opera opera
operatsiya surgery; operation
operatsiya xonasi operating
  theater
opera zali opera house
o'pka lung
oppozitsiya opposition
oq white
oq- to leak
o'q bullet
oq yo'l! bon voyage!
o'qi- to read; to study
o'qit- to teach
o'qituvchi teacher
oqsoqol (village) elder
o'quvchi student; pupil
ora interval
o'ra- to wind
o'ralgan wrapped
oraliq space
orasida among; between
o'rdak duck
o'rgan- to learn; to find out; to
  study
o'rgat- to teach
o'rgimchak spider
o'rik apricot
o'rin seat; position
o'rindiq seat
o'rish reaping
o'rmon forest
o'rnashtir- to establish

Uzbek Dictionary & Phrasebook · 41

o'rnida instead
orqa back; reverse
orqaga back; backwards
orqali through
orqasida behind
o'rta middle; center
o'rtacha average *adjective*
ortiqcha extra
ortiqcha bagaj excess baggage
o'rtoq friend; comrade
os- to hang
o's- to grow (up)
osh pilau rice
o'sha that; those
o'sha yerda there
oshpaz cook
osh qovoq pumpkin
oshqozon yarasi stomach ulcer
oshxona restaurant
o'simlik plant
osmon sky
osmondan hujum air raid
oson easy
ostanovka bus stop
ot name; horse
o't grass; herb
ot- to throw; to shoot
o't- to pass; to cross
ota ismi middle name
ota-ona parents
o'tgan past; last
o'tgan hafta last week
o'tgan yili last year
o'tgan zamon past *noun*
o'tib ket- to overtake
o'tin firewood
o'tir- to sit
o'tirish party
o'tirish taloni boarding pass
o'tkaz- to forward
o'tkir sharp
otkritka postcard
otmang! don't shoot!
ot minish horseback-riding
o't ochishni to'xtatish cease-fire
otopleniye heating; Otopleniye

o'chirildi. The heating has been cut off.
otryadlar troops
o'ttiz thirty
otvertka screwdriver
ovla- hunt
ovoz vote
ovoz ber- to vote
ovoz berish voting
ovoz berishning soxtalashtirilishi vote-rigging
ovqat food; meal; dinner; supper
ovqatlan- to dine
ovqatlanish joyi feeding station
ovqatlanish payti meal time
oxir end
oxirgi last; final
oy moon; month
oyi mother
o'yin game; play; performance
o'yla- to think
oylik pay
oyna glass; mirror
o'yna- to play; to perform
oyoq barmog'i toe
oyoq foot; leg
o'z own *adjective*
Ozarbayjon Azerbaijan
ozarbayjoncha Azeri/ Azerbaijani language
ozarbayjonlik Azeri/Azerbaijani
o'zbek Uzbek person
o'zbekcha Uzbek language
O'zbekiston Uzbekistan
o'zgartir- to alter
ozg'in thin *person*
ozgina a little bit; not much
o'zi himself; herself; itself
o'zib ket- to overtake
o'ziga xos unique
o'zim myself
o'zimiz ourselves
o'zingiz yourself
o'zinglar yourselves
ozodlik liberation; liberty

p

pakki penknife
pallos kilim; rug
palov pilau rice
palto coat; overcoat
pamil choy black tea
panoh shelter; asylum
parashyut parachute
park park
parlament parliament
parma drill
parom ferry
parovoz locomotive
paroxod boat
partiya party *political*
partizan guerrilla
pashsha fly
pasport passport; **pasport nomeri** passport number
past low
pastga down
paxta cotton
paydo bo'l- to appear
payshanba Thursday
pechat' stamp *official*
pediatr pediatrician
pediatriya pediatrics
penitsillin penicillin
peredacha gear *of car*
peredatchik transmitter
perekroystka crossing
pereval mountain pass
perron platform
perron nomeri platform number
pichoq knife
pilot pilot
pishgan ripe
pishir- to cook
pista pistachio
pistirma ambush *noun*
pitsa pizza
pivo beer
pivoxona pub
piyodaga qarshi mina anti-personnel mine
piyola Uzbek teacup
piyoz onion
plastinka record; LP
plastmassa plastic
platforma platform
plita cooker; stove
plug plow
plugshtepsel vilkasi plug *electric*
plyonka film *for camera*
pochta mail; post office
pochta yashigi mailbox
poda herd
podarka gift
podsho king; monarch
poezd train
Pokiston Pakistan
pokistonlik Pakistani
po'lat steel
poliklinika clinic
pomada lipstick; make-up
pomidor tomato
po'p priest
poraxo'rlik corruption
porla- to shine
poroshok powder
port port
portla- to explode; to blow up
portlamagan bomba unexploded bomb
portlash explosion
portlaydigan moddalar explosives
portsiya portion
posilka package; parcel
post roadblock
posyolka town
poyafzal do'koni shoe-shop
poyga horse racing
poytaxt capital city
pozitsiya position
prava driver's license
prem'yer premier
prezervativ condom
prezident president

prezident muovini vice-president
prichyoska haircut
printer printer *computer*
printsip principle
pristan dock
probka cork; stopper; bath plug
probka ochadigan corkscrew
problema problem
professional professional
professor professor
profsoyuz trade union
programma program; show
protest protest
protez artificial limb; prosthesis
proyektor projector
prujina spring *metal*
pufla- to blow
pul money; currency
pushka cannon
pushti pink

qabr grave *noun*
qabriston cemetery
qabul check-in
qabul qil- to receive
qachon? when?
qadam foot *measurement*
qadimiy ancient
qaer(da) bo'lsa ham anywhere
qahramon hero; character *in book/film*
qal'a castle; fort
qalam pencil
qalampir pepper
qalaysiz? how are you?
qalbaki counterfeit
qaldirg'och swallow *bird*
qalmoq Kalmuk
qamoq prison
qanaqa? how?; what kind?; how much?
qanaqa qilib? how?
qanchalik amount
qancha turadi? how much is it?

qand sugar cube
qanday? how?
qand kasali diabetic
qand kasalligi diabetes
qani well?
qanoatli satisfactory
qanot wing; fender
qara- to look; to watch
qarag'ay pine
qarg'a crow *bird*
qari old *people*
qarindosh relative
qarindoshlar relatives
qarmoq hook
qaror decision
qaror qil- to decide
qarz credit; debt
qarzga ber- to lend
qarzga ol- to borrow
qasam ich- to swear *an oath*
qassoblik butcher's
qatiq yogurt
qatli om massacre; ethnic cleansing
qatna- to participate
qattiq hard *not soft*
qavariq callus
qavat floor; story
qaychi scissors
qayerda? where?
qayerdan? where from?
qayir- to bend
qayna- to boil
qayoqda? where?
qaysi? which?
qayt- to return
qaytadan again
qaytadan (qil-/gapir-) to repeat
qazi horse sausage
qazi- to dig
qichi- to itch
qidir- to look for
qil body hair
qil- to do; to make
qimirla- to move
qimmat expensive
qirg'oqdan narida offshore

qo'yin

qirg'oq river bank
qirov frost
qirq forty
qish winter
qish chillasi midwinter
qishloq village
qishloqlarda in the country
qishloqlik joylar countryside
Qishloq Xo'jaligi Vazirligi
Ministry of Agriculture
qism part; section
qiyalik slope
qiyin difficult; hard
qiyma ground meat
qiymala- to grind *meat*
qiynoq torture
qiynoqla- to torture
qiz daughter
qiz bola girl
qizil red
Qizil Xoch Red Cross
qiziq interesting
qobiliyat ability
qobiq shell *of nut*
qoch- to flee; to escape; to desert
qochoq refugee; Displaced Person
qochoqlar refugees
qochoqlar lageri refugee camp
qochqin refugee; Displaced
Person
qo'chqor ram
qo'g'irchoq doll
qog'oz paper *substance*
qog'ozbozlik bureaucracy
qoida principle
qo'l hand; arm
qol- to stay; to remain
qo'l fonari flashlight
qolganlar rest; others
qo'lhunar handicraft
qo'llanma manual book
qo'l-oyoq limbs
qo'lqop gloves
qon blood
qona- to bleed
qon bosimi blood pressure
qo'ng'iroq bell

qon gruppasi blood group
qon quyish blood transfusion
qonsizlik anemia
qon tomiri vein
qonun law
qonuniy legal
qop sack
qopqon trap
qor snow; Qor yog'yapti. It is
snowing.
qora black
qora bozor black market
qorachoy Karachai
qora ko'zoynak sunglasses
qora murch black pepper
qor bo'roni blizzard
qor erishi thaw
qo'rg'on fort
qo'rg'oshin lead *metal*
qorin stomach; womb; Qornim
och. I'm hungry.; Qornim
og'riyapti. I have indigestion/
a stomachache.
qo'riqla- to protect; to guard; to
defend
qor ko'chkisi avalanche
qorong'i dark *adjective*
qorong'ilik darkness
qo'rq- to fear; to be worried
qo'rqinch fear
qo'rqit- to frighten
qo'rqmaydigan brave
qor uyumi snowdrift
qo'sh- to add
qo'shbosh pickax
qo'shinlar troops
qoshiq spoon
qo'shni neighbor
qotil killer; murderer
qotillik murder
qovun melon
qo'y sheep
qo'y- to put; mashinani qo'y-
to park a car
qo'y go'shti lamb *meat*
qo'yib yubor- to release
qo'yin lap

Uzbek Dictionary & Phrasebook · 45

qo'zi lamb *animal*
qoziq tent pegs
qozoq Kazakh
quduq well *noun*
quduq qazi- to drill a well
quduq yeri well site
qulf lock; padlock
quloq ear
qulupnay strawberry
qum sand
qur- to build
qurbaqa frog; toad
qurbon victim; martyr
qurol weapon
qurol-aslaha xazinasi arms dump
Qur'on Qur'an
qurt worm; caterpillar
qush bird
Qusyapman. I have been vomiting.
qutqar- to save; to rescue
quturish rabies
quvg'in qil- to deport
quvg'in qilish deportation
quvla- to chase
quvur tube; drain
quvvat power
quy- to pour; to pump
quyon rabbit
quyosh sun; Quyosh chiqdi. It is sunny.
quyoshdan saqlanish uchun krem sunblock cream
quyoshli sunny
quyosh turishi solstice
quyuq thick; dense

R

radar radar
radiator radiator
radio radio
radio eshittirishi radio broadcast
radioli taksi radio taxi

radio programmasi radio program
radio stantsiyasi radio station
rahbar leader
rahmat! thank you!; no thanks!
rahmat de- to thank
rak cancer
raketa missile
ramazon Ramadan
rang color
rangi so'lgan pale
rangli plyonka color film
rangsiz colorless
raqs dance
raqsga tushish dancing
rasm picture; painting; image; photo
rassom artist; painter
ratsiya walkie-talkie
rayhon basil
rayon district; region
razmer size
razvedka exploration; intelligence; spy
reaktsioner reactionary
regbi rugby
registratsiya check-in; check-in counter; reception desk
rejim regime
rejissyor film-maker
rekord record *sports*
remont repair
remont qil- to repair
rentgen X-ray
reportaj report
restoran restaurant
retsenziya review
reyls track
reys flight *plane*
reys nomeri flight number
rezinka eraser; elastic
richag lever
rok muzikasi rock 'n' roll
rok-n-rol kontserti rock concert
roman novel
ro'mol headscarf

ro'parasida preposition
Rossiya Russia
rost true
ro'yxat list
Ro'za tutyapman. I am fasting.
ro'zg'or buyumlari appliances
rubl rouble
ruchka pen; handle
rul steering wheel
rus Russian
ruscha Russian language
ruxsat ber- to allow
ryuksak backpack

S/SH

sabab reason; cause
sabzavot vegetables
sabzavot do'koni greengrocer
sabzi carrot
saf row; line
sahna stage
sakkiz eight
sakra- to leap
sakson eighty
sal: sal kam almost; **sal kam
  400 so'm** almost 400 so'm
salat lettuce; salad
salfetka napkin; tissues
salla turban
salom alaykum! hello!; *to which
  the reply is* **alaykum assalom
  (formal)** *or just* **assalomu
  alaykum**
salomka french fries
salqin cool; fresh
samolyot plane
samovar samovar
sana- to count
san'at art
san'at ko'rgazmasi art gallery
sandiq box; chest
sanoat industry
saqich chewing gum

saqla- to maintain
sarfla- to spend
sarimsoq piyoz garlic
sariq yellow; hepatitis
saroy palace
sartaroshxona barber's
sasi- to stink
sassiq kuzan ferret
savat basket
savol question
sayla- to elect
saylov election
sayohat travel
sayohat agentligi travel agent
sayohat cheklari traveler's
  checks
sayohatchi traveler; tourist
sayohat qil- to travel
sayohat qilishdan maqsad
  reason for travel
schyo't bill
sekin slow(ly); quiet(ly)
sekretar secretary
sekund second *of time*
sel flood
semir- to get fat
semiz fat *adjective*
semyachka sunflower seeds
senago'g synagogue
sentyabr September
septik septic
seriya series
seshanba Tuesday
sessiya session
sev- to love
seyf safe *box*
seysmologik tadqiqot seismic
  survey
sez- to feel
shafqatsiz cruel
shaftoli peach
shag'al gravel
shahar city
shahar markazi city center
shaharning atrofi suburb
shahar xaritasi city map
shahid martyr

shahmat chess
shakar sugar
shakl form; shape
shalola waterfall
sham candle
shamdon candlestick
shamol wind; Shamollab qoldim. I have a cold.
shamol esyapti windy
shampanskiy champagne
shampun shampoo
shanba kuni Saturday
shanba-yakshanba weekend
shapka hat
sharf scarf
sharikli (ruchka) ballpoint pen
sharob wine
sharq east *noun*
sharqiy east; eastern *adjective*
shartnoma agreement; contract
shartnomaga qo'l qo'y- to sign an agreement
shashlik shashlik
shayton devil; level *noun*
she'r poem
sherik companion
sheva dialect
shikast injury
shikastla- to injure
shikastlangan injured
shikoyat complaint
shikoyat qil- to complain
shilliq qurt snail
shim trousers
shimol north *noun*
shimoliy northern *adjective*
Shimoliy Irlandiya Northern Ireland
shina tire/tyre
shirchoy tea with milk
shirin sweet; tasty
shirinlik dessert
shirkat enterprise
shish- to swell
shisha bottle
shisha ochadigan bottle-opener

shishali clear; transparent
shkaf cupboard; cabinet
shlang hose
shofyor driver
shoh shah
shoir poet
shok shock *medical*
shokolad chocolate
shol qil- to paralyze
sho'r salty
sho'rva soup
Shoshyapman. I'm in a hurry.
Shotlandiya Scotland
shotlandiyalik Scottish person
shovqin noisy
shpion spy
shprits syringe
shtab staff
shtat state *in federation*
shtraf fine *of money*
shubhalan- to doubt
shu bilan birga besides
shunaqa similar; such
shunaqangi so
shuncha ko'p so much/many
shuningdek similar(ly)
shuning uchun therefore
shu sababdan for that reason
shu yerda here
Sibir Siberia
sichqon mouse
sidi CD
sidi pleyer CD player
sigara cigar
sigaret cigarette(s)
sigir cow
sim wire
simfoniya symphony
sindir- to break
sinf class
singil younger sister
sintaksis syntax
sir cheese; secret *noun*
sirka vinegar
sistema system
siyoh ink
siyoh rang purple

siyosat politics
siyosatchi politician
siyosatshunos political scientist
siyosiy political
siz you *singular/plural*
-siz without
sizga omad! good luck!
sizlar you *plural*
sizlarniki yours *plural*
sizlarning your
sizniki yours *singular/plural*
sizning your
sklad depot
skver main square; city/town square
snaryad shell *military*
snaryad parchasi shrapnel
S.N.B. secret police
soat hour; clock; **Soat necha bo'ldi?** What time is it?; **Soat ... bo'ldi.** It is ... o'clock.
soatsozlik watchmaker's
sobor cathedral
soch hair *on head*
soch cho'tkasi hairbrush
sochiq towel
sog' healthy; well *adjective*
sog'liq health
sog'liq xizmati healthcare
Sog'liqni Saqlash Vazirligi Ministry of Health
sohil beach; coast
so'kin- to swear; to curse
so'l(chi) left-wing
soldat soldier
soliq tax
soliq ol- to tax
soliqsiz tax-free
soliqsiz zona tax-free zone
solishtir- compare
so'm ruble
sopol idishlar pottery
so'qmoq footpath
soqol beard
soqol olish uchun krem shaving cream
so'ra- to ask

sosiska sausage
sot- to sell; to betray
sotib ol- to buy
sotoviy telefon mobile phone
sotsialist socialist
sotsializm socialism
sotuvchi salesperson
sovet council; board; soviet
Sovet Ittifoqi Soviet Union
sovg'a present; gift
sovun soap
sovuq cold *adjective*; **Sovqotib ketdim.** I am cold.
sovuq oldirish frostbite
sovuq olgan qo'l/oyoq frostbitten hands/feet
sovuq suv cold water
soy ravine
so'y- to rob
soya shade
so'z word
spalniy bedroom
spal'niy meshok sleeping bag
SPID AIDS
spirt alcohol
spirtli alcoholic *drink*
sport sports; athletics
sportchi athlete; sportsman/woman
spravochnik guidebook
sputnik satellite
sputnik telefoni satellite phone
stadion stadium
stakan glass *drinking*
stantsiya station
sterling sterling
stetoskop stethoscope
stol table; desk
stolovaya dining room
stsepleniye clutch of car
student student
stul chair
sud law court; trial
sudra- to drag
sudya judge; referee
sug'urta insurance policy
suhbat conversation

sulh peace; truce
sulton sultan
sumka bag; handbag
sun'iy artificial
sunnat circumcision
supermarket supermarket
supur- to sweep
surat picture; portrait
surgun qil- to exile
surishtir- to investigate
surishtirish investigation
surishtiruv inquiry
surma mascara
sut milk
sutemizuvchi mammal
sut fermasi dairy
sutli kofe coffee with milk
suv water; liquid; fluid; wet; **Suv to'xtab qoldi.** The water has been cut off.
suvarak cockroach
suvi qochgan stale
suvla- to wet
suvning ustida yoyilgan neft oil slick
suv shisha water bottle
suvsiz without water
suyak bone
suz- to swim
suzish swimming
svet electricity; **Svet o'chdi.** The electricity has been cut off.
svetofor traffic lights

T

tabiat nature
tabiiy natural
tabiiy boylik natural resources
tabiiy ofat natural disaster
tabletka pill; tablet
tadqiqot study; research; exploration
tag base; bottom

tagida below; under
tahlil analysis
taklifnoma invitation
taklif qil- to invite
taksi taxi
talabalar shaharchasi campus
talaffuz pronunciation
talaffuz qil- to pronounce
ta'lim education
ta'm taste
tamaki tobacco
tamg'a stamp *official*
tamom bo'l- to finish; to run out
tampon tampon
tandir tandoor oven
tanga coins
tani- to know *a person*; to recognize; **Uni taniysizmi?** Do you know him/her?
taniqli famous
tanishtir- to introduce
tank tank *military*
tanla- choose
tanosil kasalligi venereal disease
taqillat- to knock
taqriz review
taraf way
tarakan cockroach
taraqqiyot development
tarbiyali polite
tarelka plate
tariq millet
tarix history
tarixchi historian
tarjima translation
tarjima qil- to translate
tarjimai hol biography
tarjumon translator; interpreter
taroq comb
tarqal- to scatter
tarvuz watermelon
tasbeh rosary
tashi- to carry; to transport
tashkil et- to form; to found
tashkilot foundation

tashla- to quit; to throw away

tashlab ket- to quit; Tashlab ketdi. He threw it out.

Tashqi Ishlar Vazirligi Ministry of Foreign Affairs

taxminan approximately; more or less

taxta plank; board; throne

taxtakach splint *medical*

tayin certain

tayyor ready; Tayyorman. I am ready.

tayyorla- to prepare

teatr theater

tegirmon mill

teja- to save *money*

tejash economy; saving

tekis straight; level

tekshir- to check; to examine

tekshiruv punkti checkpoint

tekst text

telealoqalar telecommunications

telefon phone

telefon-avtomat public phone

telefon kodi area code

telefon qil- to telephone

telefon stantsiyasi telephone station

telegrafist telephone operator

telegramma telegram

teleks telex

telemarkaz telephone center

televidenie stantsiyasi television station

televizor television

temir iron; metal

temir yo'l railway

temperatura temperature

tennis tennis

tepa hill; top

tepaga up

tepasida on top of

ter sweat

ter-: nomer ter- to dial a number

terak poplar

teri skin; leather

terla- to sweat

termit termite

termometr thermometer

territoriya territory

teshik hole; puncture

teskari reverse *adjective*

teskarisi opposite

tez fast; quick(ly); rapid(ly)

tezlik speed

tez yordam ambulance; first aid

tibbiy medical

tibbiy sug'urta medical insurance

tijorat business; commerce

tik- to sew

tikanli sim barbed wire

tikish stitches *surgical*

tikuvchi dressmaker

til language; tongue

tilla gold

tilshunos linguist

tilshunoslik linguistics

tinch quiet *adjective*

tinchlantiruvchi tranquilizer

tinchlik peace

tinchlik muzokaralari peace talks

tinchlik saqlovchi qo'shinlar peace-keeping troops

tiniq clear

tirik alive

tirnoq finger nail

tirnoq oladigan nail-clippers

tirsak elbow

tish tooth; teeth

tish cho'tkasi toothbrush

tish doktori dentist

tish kavlagich toothpick

tishla- to bite

tish og'rig'i toothache

tish pastasi toothpaste

tizza knee

to'da flock of sheep

tog' mountain

tog'a maternal uncle

to'g'nog'ich safety pin

to'g'on dam

tog'ora basin

to'g'ri correct; right; true; direct; **To'g'ri telefon qilsa bo'ladimi?** Can I dial direct?

to'g'riga straight on; **To'g'riga yuring.** Go straight ahead.

to'g'rila- to correct

tojik Tajik

to'k- to pour out; to spill

tol willow

to'la- to pay

to'ldir- to fill; to fill in form

to'lin oy full moon

to'liq full

to'lqin wave

tom roof

tomir artery

tomoq throat

tomoq og'rig'i sore throat

tomosha qilinadigan joy sight

tong payti dawn

top- to find

to'p cannon

to'piq ankle

to'polon riot

to'pponcha pistol

topshir- to hand over

to'q dark; full

to'qqiz nine

to'q sariq orange *color*

to'qson ninety

tor narrow

to'r net

tor ko'cha sidestreet

tormoz brake

tort- to pull; to drag

to'rt four

to'rtdan bir one-quarter

to'rtdan uch three-quarters

tortib ol- to seize

to'rtinchi fourth

tortishuv dispute; feud

tortma drawer

tosh rock; stone

to'siq fence

tos suyagi pelvis

tost toast

tot- to taste

tovuq chicken; hen

tovush voice; sound; noise

to'xta- to stop; **to'xtamang!** don't stop!

toychoq pony

To'yib ketdim! I am full!

toza clean; **toza suv** drinking water

tozala- to clean

tozalash xizmati room service

traktor tractor

transformator transformer

travma trauma

trolleybus trolley bus

tromboz thrombosis

tros tow rope

truba tube

trubka handset; pipe

tsar tsar

tsentr city center; town center

tsigan European Gypsy

tsitrus citrus

tualet bathroom; toilet; **Tualet ishlamayapti.** The toilet won't flush.

tualet(lar) toilet(s)

tufayli because of

tufla- to spit

tufli shoes

tug'- to give birth (to)

tuga- to run out; **Benzin tugadi.** I have run out of gas.

tugat- to consume

tug'ilgan joy place of birth

tug'ilgan kun date of birth

tug'ilish birth

tug'ilish guvohnomasi birth certificate

tuk hair *on body*

tuman mist; fog

tumanli misty

tuman tushgan foggy

tunnel tunnel

tur type

tur- to get up; to stand; to stay *in*

one place; to rise; to live *somewhere;* to wake
turist tourist
turizm tourism
turizm idorasi tourist office
turk Turk
turkcha Turkish
Turkiya Turkey
Turmushqa chiqmaganman. I am single. *said by a woman*
Turmushqa chiqqanman. I am married. *said by a woman*
turna crane *bird*
turniket tourniquet
tush dream *noun*
tush- to fall
tushdan keyin afternoon; p.m.
tushlik lunch
tushun- to understand; Tushunaman. I understand.; Tushunmadim. I don't understand.
tushuntir- to explain; to describe
tushuntirish explanation
tush vaqti noon
tut mulberry
tut- to arrest
tutqanoq epileptic
tutqanoq kasalligi epilepsy
tutqun prisoner
tutun smoke
tuxum egg
tuya camel
tuyg'u feeling; sense
tuz salt
tuzal- to heal
Tuzalib qoldim. I feel better.
tuzat- to correct; to fix; to repair; to treat
tuzoq booby trap
tuzum structure

U

u he; she; it; that; **u taraf** that way

u(ni) her; him; it
uch three; **uch marta** three times; thrice
uch- to fly
uchar likopcha UFO
uchdan bir one-third
uchdan ikki two-thirds
uchinchi third *adjective*
uchish maydonchasi landing strip
uchrash- to meet
Uels Wales
uelslik Welsh
uka younger brother
Ukraina Ukraine
ukraincha Ukrainian language
ukrop dill
uksus vinegar
ulab ber- to transfer/put through *on the phone*
ular they
ularniki theirs
ularning their
ularning o'zi themselves
ulug' great
ulush portion; share
umivalnik sink; basin
umumiy general *adjective*
umurtqa spine; back
un flour
unchalik sovuq bo'lmagan qish mild winter
uniki his; hers; its
universitet college; university
unts ounce
unumli fertile
ur- to hit; to beat
urf-odat custom; tradition
urg'ochi female *animal*
urug' seed
urush war
urush- to wage war
urush qoidalariga qarshi jinoyat war crime
urush tribunali war tribunal
ushla- to hold; to catch
uslub technique

ust top
ustida on; onto
usul fashion
uvishib qol- to have pins and
needles
uxla- to sleep
uy house
uyal- to be ashamed
uyali telefon mobile phone
uy egasi host
uyg'on- to wake
uyg'oq awake
uyg'otish uchun telefon wake-
up call
Uylanganman. I am married.
said by a man
uyqi sleep
uyqi dori sleeping pill(s)
Uyqim kelyapti. I am sleepy.
uysiz homeless
uyushtir- to arrange
Uzildi. I've been cut off.
uzoq distant; far
uzr apology; **uzr!** I apologize!
uzuk ring
uzum grape
uzun long

V

va and
vabo cholera
vagon-restoran dining car
vakil representative
vakil bo'l- to represent
vakillik representation
vaqt time
vaqtida on time
vaqtli early
varenye raspberry
vatan homeland
vayron qil- to ravage
vaza vase
vazir minister
vazirlik ministry

vaziyat situation
Vegeterianman. I am a vegetarian.
velosiped bicycle
ventilyator fan
ventilyator qayishi fan belt
vertolyot helicopter
veto veto
videokasseta video cassette
videomagnitofon video player
viklyuchatel switch *electric*
vilka fork
vino wine
vint screw
virus virus
vishka derrick
viski whisky
vitse prezident vice-president
vixlop car exhaust
viza visa
vodiy valley
vokzal train station
voltaj voltage
voz kech- to withdraw; to give up
vspishka *camera* flash

X

xabarlar news
xachir mule
xafa sad; unhappy; **Xafa
bo'ldim.** I am annoyed. *or*
I am sad.
xalq folk
xalq muzikasi folk music
xalq raqslari folk dancing
Xalq Ta'limi Vazirligi Ministry
of Education
xalqaro kod international code
xalqaro reys international flight
xalqaro telegrafist international
operator
xanjar dagger
xarakter character
xarita map

xaroba ruins
xashak hay
xat letter; message
xato mistake
xato qil- to make a mistake
xavf danger
xavflilik risk
xavfsiz safe *adjective*
xavfsizlik safety; security
xavf-xatarli treacherous
xavotir ol- to be worried
xayr! good-bye!
xazina treasury
xil kind; type; sort
ximiya chemistry
ximiyaviy modda chemical
xirurg surgeon
xitoy Chinese
xizmat service
xodim office worker
xodimlar staff
xohla- to desire
xohlagan joyingiz anywhere
xohlagan odam anyone
xo'jalik mollari do'koni hard-ware store
xo'jalik qog'ozi toilet paper
xo'jayin husband; boss
xolodilnik fridge
xom raw
xom neft crude oil
xona room
xona nomeri room number
xo'p! no problem!
xo'r choir
xo'roz rooster
xotin female *adjective*
xotin kishi woman; wife; female
xotin podsho queen
xotira memory
xristiyan Christian
xristiyan dini Christianity
xrustal crystal
xuddi exact
Xudo God
xurmo date *fruit*; persimmon
xursand happy

Y

yadro energiyasi nuclear power; nuclear energy
yadro quroliga ega davlat nuclear power *political*
yadro stantsiyasi nuclear power station/plant
yagona unique
yahudiy Jewish
yahudiy dini Judaism
yakshanba Sunday
yalpizli menthol
yana again
yana bir another
yanch- to grind *grain*
yangi new; fresh
yangi oy new moon
yangi yil New Year *January 1*
Yangizilandiya New Zealand
yanvar January
yapon Japanese
yaponcha Japanese language
Yaponiya Japan
yaqin near (-**ga** to); nearby
yaqinda recently; soon
yara injury; wound
yarala- to injure; to wound
yaralangan injured
yard yard *distance*
yarim half
yarim kecha midnight
yasa- to create; to form
yasha- to dwell; to live; to be alive
yashil green
yashin lightning
yaxshi good; fine; nice; excellent; kind
yaxshi bo'l- to improve
yaxshi dam oling(lar)! good night!
yaxshi ko'radigan qiz girlfriend
yaxshi ko'radigan yigit boyfriend

yaxshilan-

yaxshilan- to improve
yaxshiroq better
yaxshiroq ko'r- to prefer
ye- to eat; to consume
yech- to undo
yelim pitch
yelka shoulder
yeng- to defeat; to conquer
yengil light *not heavy*
yer land; earth; floor; ground; place; space
yer hayda- to plow
yer ko'chkisi landslide
yer och- to clear land
yer tagida underground
yerto'la basement; cellar
yetarli enough; satisfactory
yetarli emas not enough
yetim orphan
yetmish seventy
yetti seven
Yevropa Europe
Yevropa Ittifoqi European Union
yevropalik European *adjective*
yigirma twenty
yig'la- to cry; to weep
yil year
yiqil- to fall
yiring (lagan joy) infection
yirt- to tear
yirtiq joy tear
yodgor souvenir
yodgorlik monument
yog' cooking oil; fat
yog' bankasi oilcan
yog'ingarchilik rainy weather
yog'och wood *substance*
yoki or
yo'l path; road; route; way; footpath
yo'l ber- to yield
yo'l ko'rsat- to guide
yo'l xaritasi road map
yo'ldosh companion
yolg'iz alone
yolg'on lie

yollanma askar mercenary
yollanma qotil assassin
yo'llar kesishgan joy crossroads
yo'lovchi passenger; traveler
yo'l-yo'riq directions
yomg'ir rain; yomg'ir yog'yapti it is raining
yomon bad; badly
yomon ko'r- to hate
yomonroq worse; Yomonroq his qilyapman. I feel worse.
yomon yurak heart condition
yon- to burn
yo'nat- to transmit
yong'oq walnut
yonida beside
yonilg'i fuel
yonilg'i bazasi fuel dump
yop- to close/shut
yopiq closed/shut
yopish- to stick
yoq- to light; to switch on; to set fire to
yo'q no; there is/are not
yoqa shore
yo'qot- to lose; Kalitimni yo'qotib qo'ydim. I have lost my key.
yo'q qil- to destroy
yor- to split
yordam help; aid; relief aid
yordam ber- to help; yordam beringlar! help!
yoril- to burst
yorug'lik o'lchaydigan apparat light meter
yosh young; age; Yoshingiz nechada? How old are you?; ... yoshdaman. I am ... years old.
yosh bola young person
yoshlantiruvchi gaz tear gas
yostiq pillow
yot- to lie down; to go to bed
yo'tal- to cough
yotiladigan joy accommodation

yotoq vagon sleeping car
yotoqxona bedroom
yotqiz- to lay
yovvoy wild
yoy- to spread
yoz summer
yoz- to write; to record
yoz chillasi midsummer
yozuv writing; sign; inscription
yozuvchi writer
yubor- to end; to transmit
yugurdak courier
yuk cargo; freight
yuk bo'limi baggage counter
yuksak qon bosimi high blood
  pressure
yuk yubor- to freight; to ship
yulduz star
yumor humor
yumshoq soft
yuqoriga up
yuqtir- to transmit
yur- to go
yurak heart
yuring! go!
yut- to swallow
yutqiz- to lose *a game*
yuv- to wash
yuz face; hundred

Z

zabastovka strike *from work*
zabastovka qil- to strike *from*

work
zachyot final *noun*
za'faron saffron
zag'izxon magpie
zahar poison
zajigalka lighter
zakaz xat registered mail
zambarak cannon
zambil stretcher
zamonaviy modern; contemporary
zang rust
zanjir chain
zapas extra; reserves; supply;
  zapas shina spare tire
zapas adyol an extra blanket
zararli harmful
zargarlik buyumlari jewelry
zavod factory
zilzila earthquake
zira cumin
zirak earrings
zirak-uzuk jewelry
ziyofat banquet
ziyoratchi pilgrim
ziyoratgoh shrine; saint's
  tomb
zontik umbrella
zoopark zoo
zor orchard *suffix*
zo'ravonlik violence
zo'rla- to rape; **Meni bittasi
  zo'rladi.** I've been raped.
zvochka chewing gum
zvukoapparatura sound equipment

ENGLISH–UZBEK
INGLIZCHA-O'ZBEKCHA

A

ability qobiliyat
Abkhaz abxaz
Abkhazia Abxaziya
able: to be able -a ol-; I am able to go. Bora olaman.
about... ...haqida
academic akademik
academy akademiya; **academy of sciences** fanlar akademiyasi
accelerator gaz pedali
accent aksent
access: Do you have access for the disabled? Nogironlar uchun sharoitlar bormi?
accident avariya *vehicle*; There's been an accident. Avariya bo'ldi.
accommodation yotiladigan joy
according to... ...ga ko'ra
accountant buxgalter
accuse aybla-
activist faol; aktivist
actor artist
actual haqiqiy, rostakam
adapter adaptor
add qo'sh-
addition: in addition to bilan birga
address adres
administrator administrator
admiral admiral
adventure sarguzasht; boshdan kechirganlar
Afghan afg'on
Afghanistan Afg'oniston
afraid: to be afraid of ...-dan qo'rq-

after ...-dan keyin
afternoon tushdan/obeddan keyin; **this afternoon** bugun obeddan keyin
afterwards keyinroq
again qaytadan; yana
age yosh
ago ...(dan) oldin
agreement shartnoma; **to sign an agreement** shartnomaga qo'l qo'y-
agriculture dehqonchilik
agronomist agronom
aid yordam; **humanitarian aid** insonparvarlik yordami; **first aid** tez yordam
aid worker beg'araz yordam ko'rsatuvchi
AIDS SPID
air havo
air base aviabaza
air conditioner konditsionir
air conditioning konditsionir sistemasi
air force harbiy havo kuchlari
air mail aviaxat
air raid osmondan hujum
airline havo yo'llari
airplane samolyot
airport aeroport
airport tax aeroport solig'i
alcohol spirt
alcoholic: *substance* spirtli; *person* aroqxo'r
alcoholism aroqxo'rlik
alive tirik
all hamma
all together hamma birga

allergic: I'm allergic to... ...ga allergiyam bor
allergy allergiya
allow ruxsat ber-
almost deyarli; sal kam; ...ga oz qoldi; **almost 400 so'm** sal kam 400 so'm; **I almost died.** O'lishimga oz qoldi.
alone yolg'iz
alphabet alifbo
already: I've already seen that film. U kinoni ko'rib bo'ldim.
also ham
alter o'zgartir-
although bo'lsa ham
altitude sickness balandlik kasalligi
always har doim
a.m. ertalab
ambassador elchi
ambulance tez yordam
ambush *noun* pistirma
America Amerika
American amerikalik
among orasida
amount qanchalik; ko'plik
amputation amputatsiya
analysis tahlil
ancestor ajdod
ancient qadimiy
and bilan; ham; va *in written Uzbek*; **both... and...** ham..., ham...
anemia qonsizlik
anesthetic og'riq qoldiruvchi
anesthetist anesteziolog
angle burchak
angry jahli chiqqan
animal hayvon
ankle to'piq
annoyed: I am annoyed. Xafa bo'ldim.; Jonimga tegdi.
another yana bir
answer javob
ant chumoli
antibiotic antibiotik
anti-freeze antifriz

anti-personnel mine piyodaga qarshi mina
antiseptic antiseptik
anti-vehicle mine mashinalarga qarshi mina
anyone kim bo'lsa ham; xohlagan odam
anywhere qaer(da) bo'lsa ham; xohlagan joyingiz
apartment kvartira
apartment complex dom
apologize: I apologize! Uzr!
apology uzr
appear paydo bo'l-; kel-
appendicitis apenditsit
apple olma
appliances ro'zg'or buyumlari
approximately taxminan
apricot o'rik
April aprel
Arab arab
Arabic *language* arabcha
Aral Sea Orol dengizi
archaeological arxeologik
archaeology arxeologika
architect arxitekt; me'mor
architecture arxitektura
area atrof
area code telefon kodi
arm qo'l
Armenia Armaniston
Armenian arman
armored car bronemashina
arms dump qurol-aslaha xazinasi
army armiya
arrange uyushtir-
arrest tut-; qo'lga ol-
arrivals kelish jadvali
arrive kel-
art san'at
art gallery san'at ko'rgazmasi
artery tomir
article maqola
artificial sun'iy
artificial limb protez
artillery artillerya
artist rassom

ashamed: to be ashamed uyal-
ashtray kuldon
ask so'ra-
aspirin aspirin
assassin yollanma qotil
assassination suiqasd qilib o'ldirish
assembly majlis
asthma astma
asthmatic astmali
at -da
at least eng kamida
athlete sportchi
athletics sport; atletika
atlas atlas
attack *noun* hujum; *verb* hujum qil-
August avgust
Australia Avstraliya
Australian avstraliyalik
author avtor; muallif
auto spares store zapchast; ehtiyot qismlar do'koni
autonomous avtonom; muxtor
autonomy avtonomiya; muxtorlik
autumn kuz
avalanche qor ko'chkisi
average *adjective* o'rtacha
awake uyg'oq
ax bolta
Azerbaijan Ozarbayjon
Azeri, Azerbaijani ozarbayjonlik; *language* ozarbayjoncha

B

baby go'dak; chaqaloq
back *adverb* orqaga
back *noun* orqa; bel
backache bel og'rig'i
backpack ryuksak
backwards orqaga
bacteria bakteriya

bad yomon
badly yomon
bag sumka
baggage bagaj; **excess baggage** ortiqcha bagaj
baggage counter bagaj kamerasi; yuk bo'limi
bake duxovkada pishir-
baker's; bakery novvoyxona
balcony balkon
Balkar Balkar
ball koptok
ballet balet
ballpoint sharikli (ruchka)
Band-Aid leykoplastir
bandit bandit; o'g'ri
bank bank; **river bank** qirg'oq
banker bankir
bank note banknot
banquet ziyofat
bar bar
barbed wire tikanli sim
barber's sartaroshxona
bark *verb* akilla-
barley arpa
barn og'il
barracks barak
barrel barrel (oil)
barren bo'sh
bartender barmen
base tag; asos
basement yerto'la
basil rayhon
basin tog'ora
basis asos
basket savat
basketball basketbol
bathe cho'mil-
bathroom tualet; hojatxona; hammom
battery batareya; *of car* akkumulyator
battle jang
bay ko'rfaz
be bo'l-
beach sohil
beans loviya

border

bear ayiq
beard soqol
beat ur-; *sports* yut-
beautiful chiroyli
beauty go'zallik
beauty parlor ayollar sar-taroshxonasi
because chunki
because of ...dan; tufayli
become bo'l-
bed karavot; **to go to bed** yot-
bedroom spalniy; yotoqxona
bee ari
beef mol go'shti
beer pivo
beetroot lavlagi
before ...dan oldin
begin boshla-
beginning bosh
behind orqasida
believe ishon-
bell qo'ng'iroq
below tagida
belt kamar
bend in road burilish
bend *verb* qayir-
berry: mulberry tut; **raspberry** varenye; **strawberry** qulupnay
beside yonida
besides shu bilan birga
best eng yaxshi
betray sot-
better yaxshiroq; **I feel better.** Tuzalib qoldim.
between orasida
Bible injil
bicycle velosiped
big katta
biggest eng katta
bill schyo't
binoculars durbin
biography tarjimai hol
bird qush
birth tug'ilish; **to give birth to** tug'-
birth certificate tug'ilish guvohnomasi
birth control homiladorlikdan saqlanish (vositalari)
bishop episkop
bit; a little bit ozgina
bite tishla-
bitter achchiq
black qora
black market qora bozor
blanket adyol
bleed qona-
blind ko'r
blizzard qor bo'roni
blocked: The toilet is blocked. Tualetda suv tiqilib qoldi.
blood qon
blood group qon gruppasi
blood pressure qon bosimi; davlenie
blood transfusion qon quyish
blow pufla-
blow up portla-
blue ko'k
blues blyuz
board *council* sovet; kengash
boarding pass o'tirish taloni
boat paroxod
body badan
boil *noun* chipqon; *verb* qayna-
bomb bomba
bomb disposal bomba zarar-sizlantirish
bombardment bombardimon
bomber bombardirovkachi
bon appetit! olinglar!
bon voyage! oq yo'l!
bone suyak
bonnet *of car* kapot
booby trap tuzoq
book kitob
bookshop kitob do'koni
boot etik
boot *of car* bagaj joyi
boots etik; *soleless leather boots* mahsi
border chegara

border crossing chegara punkti
border guard chegarachi
born: Where were you born?
  Qayerda tug'ilgansiz?; **I was
  born in ... ...**da tug'ilganman.
borrow qarzga ol-
boss xo'jayin
both ikkovi
both ... and ham ... ham ...
bottle shisha; **bottle of beer**
  bitta pivo; **bottle of water** bir
  shisha suv; **bottle of wine** bir
  shisha vino
bottle-opener shisha ochadigan
bottom tag
bowl kosa
box karobka
boxing boks
boy o'g'il bola
boyfriend yaxshi ko'radigan yigit
bracelet bilaguzuk
brake tormoz
brandy konyak
brave qo'rqmaydigan; jur'atli
bread non
break *verb* sindir-
**break down: Our car has
  broken down.** Mashinamiz
  buzilib qoldi.
break for refreshments dam
  olish uchun tanaffus
breakfast (ertalabki) choy
breast ko'krak
breath nafas
breed *verb* ko'pay(tir)-
brick g'isht
bridge ko'prik
bring olib kel-
Britain Britaniya
British britaniyalik
brooch broshka
brother: *younger* uka; *older* aka
brown jigarrang
bruise *verb* ko'kartir-
brush cho'tka
bucket chelak
Buddhism buddo dini

Buddhist buddist
budget byudjet
build qur-
building bino
bull buqa
bullet o'q
bumper amortizator
bureaucracy qog'ozbozlik
burn yon-; *to set fire to* yoq-
burst yoril-
bury ko'm-
bus avtobus
bus station avtostantsiya
bus stop ostanovka; bekat
business *firm* firma; *commerce*
  tijorat
business class biznes klas
businessman/woman biznesmen
busy: The line is busy. Band.
but lekin
butane canister gaz baloni
butcher's qassoblik
butterfly kapalak
buy sotib ol-

C

cabbage karam
cabinet shkaf
cable kabel
calculator kalkulyator
calf *cow* buzoq
call chaqir-; telefon qil-; **Call
  the police.** Militsiyaga telefon
  qiling.
called: What are you called?
  Ismingiz nima?; **I'm called
  Fred.** Ismim Fred.; **What is
  this called?** Buni nima deysi-
  zlar?
callus qavariq
camel tuya
camera fotoapparat
camera equipment fotoapparat

jihozlari

camp: Can we camp here? Shu yerda chodir qurish bo'ladimi?

camping chodir qurish

campsite chodir tikiladigan joy

campus talabalar shaharchasi

can *noun* banka; *& see* **able**

can opener banka ochadigan

Canada Kanada

Canadian kanadalik

canal kanal

cancel bekor qil-; **The plane is cancelled.** Reys bekor qilindi.

cancer rak

candle sham

candlestick shamdon

candy konfet

canister banka

cannon pushka; to'p; zambarak

capital *financial* kapital

capital city poytaxt

car mashina

car papers mashina dokumentlari ; hujjatlari

car park mashina to'xtash joyi

car registration mashina registratsiyasi

car spares store zapchast; ehtiyot qislmar do'koni

caravan karvon

care *noun* ehtiyotlik; *verb* boq-

careful ehtiyot

cargo yuk

carpenter duradgor

carpet gilam

carrier bag katta sumka

carrot sabzi

carry olib yur-; tashi-

cart aravacha

carton of cigarettes bir karton sigaret

cashier kassir

cashier's booth kassa

casino kazino

Caspian Sea Kaspiy dengizi

cassette kasseta

castle qal'a

cat mushuk

catch ushla-

caterpillar qurt

cathedral sobor

Catholic katolik

cattle mol

Caucasus Kavkaz

cause sabab

cave g'or

caviar ikra

CD sidi

CD player sidi pleyer

ceasefire o't ochishni to'xtatish

cellar yerto'la

cemetery qabriston

center o'rta; markaz

Central Asia O'rta Osiyo

century asr

ceramics keramika

certain tayin; aniq

certainly albatta

chain zanjir

chair stul

champagne shampanskiy

change: I want to change some dollars. Dollar almashtirmoqchiman.

channel kanal

chapter bob

character xarakter; *in book/film* qahramon

charge: What is the charge? Qancha bo'ladi?; **Who is in charge?** Kim boshliq qilyapti?

charity *organization* beg'araz yordam tashkiloti

chase quvla-

cheap arzon

cheaper arzonroq

Chechen chechen

Chechnya Chechnya

check *money* chek; *verb* tekshir-; **Could you please check the bill again?** Qaytadan hisoblab ko'rolasizmi?; **Check the oil please.** Yog'ni tekshirib boqing.

check-in registratsiya; qabul

check-in counter registratsiya
checkpoint tekshiruv punkti
cheers! sog'liq uchun!
cheese sir
chemical ximiyaviy modda
chemistry ximiya
chess shahmat
chest *human* ko'krak; *box* sandiq
chew chayna-
chewing gum zvochka; saqich
chicken tovuq
chief bosh(liq)
child bola
children bolalar
chimney mo'ri
chin iyak
Chinese xitoy
chocolate shokolad
choir xo'r
choke bo'g'il-; He is choking. Bo'g'ilyapti.
cholera vabo
choose tanla-
chop chop-
Christian xristiyan
Christianity xristiyan dini
Christmas archa bayrami (= *New Year*)
church cherkov
cigar sigara
cigarette(s) sigaret
cigarette papers maxorka qog'ozi
cinema kino; kinoteatr
Circassian cherkez
circle doira
circumcision sunnat
citizen fuqaro
citizenship fuqarolik
citrus tsitrus
city shahar
city center shahar markazi; tsentr
city hall gorispolkom
city map shahar xaritasi
civil rights fuqaro huquqlari
civil war fuqarolar urushi
civilian fuqaro

class sinf
classical music klassik muzika
clean *adjective* toza; **clean sheets** toza choyshab; *verb* tozala-
clear *adjective: sky/water* tiniq; *plastic* shishali; *verb:* **to clear land** yer och-; **to clear mines** mina zararsizlantir-
climate iqlim
clinic poliklinika
clock soat
close yop-; What time does it close? Qachon yopiladi?
closed yopiq
clothes kiyim
clothes shop kiyim-kechak magazini
cloud bulut
cloudy: It's cloudy. Havo bulut.
clown masxaraboz
club klub
clutch *of car* stsepleniye
coal ko'mir
coal mine ko'mir koni
coast sohil; bo'y
coat palto; *Uzbek coat* chopon
cockroach tarakan; suvarak
code kod; **international code** xalqaro kod
coffee kofe; **coffee with milk** sutli kofe
cognac konyak; brandy
coins tanga
cold *adjective* sovuq; **cold water** sovuq suv; **it is cold** havo sovuq; **I am cold,** Sovqotib ketdim.; **I have a cold.** Shamollab qoldim.
colleague hamkasb
collective farm kolxoz
college kolledj; institut; universitet
color rang
color film rangli plyonka
colorless rangsiz
comb taroq

combine harvester kombayn
come kel-
come in! keling!; kiring!
commission komissiya
commission: What is the commission? Qancha ob qolinadi?
communications aloqalar
communism kommunizm
Communist kommunist
community jamoat; *of city* mahalla
companion sherik; yo'ldosh
compare solishtir-
compass kompas
compensation haq
competition konkurs
complain shikoyat qil-
complaint shikoyat
composer kompozitor; bastakor
composition kompozitsiya; asar
computer kompyuter
comrade o'rtoq
concentration camp kontslager
concert kontsert
concert hall kontsert zali
concussion *medical* kontuziya
condition ahvol; hol
condom prezervativ
conference konferentsiya
conference room konferentsiya zali
confuse bosh aylantir-
connection aloqa
conquer yeng-
constipation: I have constipation. Ichim qotib qoldi.
constitution konstitutsiya
consulate konsulxona
consultant konsul'tant
consume ye-; tugat-
contact: I want to contact my embassy. Elchixonamga telefon qilmoqchiman.
contact lenses kontakt linza

contact lens solution kontakt linza saqlanadigan suyuqlik
contain ighiga ol-
container *freight* konteyner
contemporary zamonaviy
contest musobaqa
continue davom et-
contract kontrakt; shartnoma
control boshqar-
conversation suhbat
convoy konvoy
cook *noun* oshpaz; *verb* pishir-
cooker plita
cool *air* salqin; *drink* muzday
co-operation hamkorlik
copper mis
copse daraxtzor
copy *noun* kseroks; fotokopiya; *verb* ko'chir-; kseroks qil-
coriander kashnich
corkscrew probka ochadigan
cork stopper probka
corn makka jo'xori
corner burchak
correct *adjective* to'g'ri; *verb* tuzat-; to'g'rila-
corruption korruptsiya; poraxo'rlik
cost narx; How much does this cost? Mana bu qancha turadi?; Necha pul?
cotton paxta
cotton wool paxta
cough yo'tal-
council sovet; kengash
count *verb* sana-
counterfeit qalbaki; This money is counterfeit. Bu pul qalbaki ekan.
country mamlakat; in the country qishloqlarda
countryside qishloqlik joylar
coup d'etat davlat to'ntarilishi
courier kur'er; yugurdak
court *law* sud
courtyard hovli
cow sigir

craftsman

craftsman hunarmand
crane *machine* kran; *bird* turna
crash avariya
crazy jinni
create yasa-; ijod qil-
credit kredit; qarz
credit card kredit kartochkasi
crime jinoyat
criminal jinoyatchi
crisis krizis; ofat
crops ekinlar
cross *verb* o't-
crossing perekroystka; kechuv; dovon
crossroads yo'llar kesishgan joy
crow *bird* qarg'a
crude oil xom neft
cruel shafqatsiz
cry yig'la-
crystal xrustal
cucumber bodring
culture madaniyat
cumin zira
cup chashka; *handleless teacup* piyola
cupboard shkaf
cure *noun* davo; *verb* davola-
currency pul
custom *tradition* urf-odat
customs *border* bojxona
cut kes-; **The lines have been cut.** Simlar uzilgan.
cut off: **I've been cut off.** Uzildi.; **The electricity has been cut off.** Svet o'chdi.; **The gas has been cut off.** Gaz o'chdi.; **The heating has been cut off.** Otopleniye o'chirildi.; **The water has been cut off.** Suv to'xtab qoldi.

D

dagger xanjar
Daghestan Dog'iston

Daghestani dog'istonlik
dairy sut fermasi
dam to'g'on
dance *noun* raqs
dancing raqsga tushish
danger xavf
Danish daniyalik
dark *adjective* qorong'i; to'q (color); *noun* qorong'ilik
darkness qorong'ilik
date chislo; kun
date *fruit* xurmo; **What date is it today?** Bugun chislo necha?
date of arrival kelish muddati
date of birth tug'ilgan kun
date of departure ketish muddati
daughter qiz
dawn *noun* tong payti
day kun
daytime kunduz
dead o'lgan
deaf kar
dear *loved* aziz
death o'lim
debt qarz
decade o'n yil
December dekabr
decide qaror qil-
decision qaror
deep chuqur
deep-water platform katta chuqurlikdagi platfo'rma
deer kiyik
defeat *verb* yeng-
defend qo'riqla-
delay kechiktir-
delayed: **The plane is delayed.** Samolyo't kechikadi.
democracy demokratiya
democratic demokratik
demonstration *political* namoyish
demonstrators *political* namoyishchilar
dentist tish doktori
deodorant dezodorant

down

department idora; bo'lim
department store katta magazin
departures ketish jadvali
depend: It depends. Har xil.
deport quvg'in qil-
deportation quvg'in qilish
depot ombor; sklad
deprive mahrum qil-
derivative *noun* hosila
derrick vishka
describe tushuntir-
desert *noun* cho'l
desert *verb* qoch-
desire *verb* xohla-; ista-
desk stol
dessert shirinlik; desert
destroy yo'q qil-
detergent kir yuvish poroshogi
development taraqqiyot
devil shayton
diabetes qand kasalligi
diabetic qand kasali
diagnosis diagnoz
dial (a number) (nomer) ter-
dialect sheva
dialing code kod
diarrhea: I have diarrhea.
    Ichim ketyapti.
dictator diktator
dictatorship diktatorlik
dictionary lug'at
die o'l-
diesel dizel
diet dieta
different boshqa; farqli
difficult qiyin
dig qazi-
digital digital
dill ukrop
dine ovqatlan-
dining car vagon-restoran
dining room stolovaya
dinner (kechki) ovqat
diplomat elchi
diplomatic ties diplomatik aloqalar
direct to'g'ri; bevosita; **Can I
    dial direct?** To'g'ri telefon

qilsa bo'ladimi?
directions yo'l-yo'riq
directory adres daftari
dirty kir; iflos
disabled nogiron
disaster ofat; **natural disaster**
    tabiiy ofat
disco diskoteka
discover kashf et-
discuss haqida gaplash-; mulo-
    haza qil-
discussion mulohaza
disease kasallik
disk-jockey disk jokey
Displaced Person qochqin
dispute tortishuv
dissolve eri-
distant uzoq
district rayon
ditch ariq
diver g'avvos
divide bo'l-
divorced er/xotini bilan ajrashgan
divorced: I am divorced. *said
    by a man* Xotinim bilan ajrash-
    ganman.; *said by a woman* Erim
    bilan ajrashganman.
dizzy: I feel dizzy. Boshim
    aylanyapti.
do qil-
dock pristan
doctor doktor
document dokument; hujjat
documentary film hujjatli film
dog kuchuk; it
doll qo'g'irchoq
dollar dollar
dome gumbaz
donkey eshak
door eshik
doorlock qulf
double: double bed ikki kishilik
    karavot; **double room** ikki
    kishilik xona
doubt shubhalan-; ishonma-
dove musicha
down pastga

drag

drag sudra-; tort-
drain quvur
draw chiz-
drawer tortma
dream *noun* tush
dress *noun* ko'ylak; *Uzbek silk
dress* atlas ko'ylak
dressed: to get dressed kiyin-
dressmaker tikuvchi
drill *noun* parma
drill a well quduq qazi-
drilling parma bilan qazi-
drink *noun* ichimlik; *verb* ich-
drinking water toza suv
drive hayda-
driver shofyor
driver's license prava
drug dori; *narcotic* narkotik
drug addict narkoman; giyohvand
drum nog'ora
drunk mast
duck o'rdak
during davomida
Dutch gollandiyalik
duty: customs duty boj
dwell yasha-
dynamo dinamo

E

each har bitta
each other bir-biri
eagle burgut
ear quloq
early vaqtli
earrings zirak
earth yer
earthquake zilzila
east *noun* sharq
east(ern) *adjective* sharqiy
easy oson
eat ye-
economics iqtisod; ekonomika
economist iqtisodchi; ekonomist
economy *of country* iqtisod;

saving tejash
editor muharrir
education ta'lim; maorif
egg tuxum
eight sakkiz
eighteen o'n sakkiz
eighty sakson
elbow tirsak
elder; village elder oqsoqol
elect sayla-
election saylov
electrical goods store elektron
buyumlar do'koni
electricity svet; elektr
elevator lift
eleven o'n bir
e-mail elektron pochta
e-mail address elektron pochta
adresi
embassy elchixona
emergency favqulodda holat
emergency exit avariya holatida
chiqish
empty *adjective* bo'sh; *verb*
bo'shat-
enamel emal
end *noun* oxir; *verb* bitir-
enemy dushman
engine motor
engineer injener
England Angliya
English ingliz; *language*
inglizcha
enough yetarli; **That's enough,
thanks.** Bo'ldi, rahmat.
enquiry surishtiruv
enter kir-
enterprise shirkat
entire butun
entrance kirish
envelope konvert
epidemic epidemiya
epilepsy tutqanoq kasalligi;
epilepsiya
epileptic tutqanoq
equipment asbob-uskunalar;
jihozlar

-er/-est ...roq; eng ...
era davr
eraser rezinka
escalator eskalator
escape qoch-
especially ayniqsa
essay ocherk
establish o'rnashtir-
ethnic cleansing qatli om; milliy qirg'in; etnik tozalash
etiquette odob
Europe Yevropa
European *adjective* yevropalik
European Union Yevropa Ittifoqi
evening kechqurun; kechki payt
every har (bir)
everybody/everyone hamma
every day har kuni
everything hamma narsa
evidence isbot
exact aniq; xuddi
exam imtihon
examine tekshir-
example misol
excellent juda yaxshi; a'lo
except (for) ... ...-dan boshqa
excess ortiqcha
exchange almashtir-
exchange rate: What's the exchange rate? Kurs qancha?
excluded ichiga kirmaydi
excuse *noun* bahona
excuse me! Kechirasiz!
execute o'lim jazosiga hukm qil-
execution o'ldirish; o'lim jazosi
executioner jallod
exercise *noun* badan tarbiya; fizkultura
exhaust *of car* vixlop
exhibit *verb* ko'rsat-
exhibition ko'rgazma
exile surgun qil-
exit chiqish
expect kut-
expel chiqar-
expensive qimmat

explain tushuntir-
explanation tushuntirish; javob
explode portla-
exploration tadqiqot; razvedka
explosion portlash
explosives portlaydigan moddalar
export *noun* eksport; *verb* eksport qil-
express *fast* ekspress; *verb* ayt-
extend cho'z-
extra ortiqcha; zapas; **an extra blanket** zapas adyol
eye ko'z
eyeglasses ko'zoynak; ochki
eyesight ko'z (ko'rish qobiliyati)

F

face yuz; bet
fact fakt
factory zavod; fabrika
failure muvaffaqiyatsizlik
fall *autumn* kuz
fall *verb* tush-; yiqil-
fallowland bo'sh qolgan dala
false noto'g'ri
family oila
famous mashhur; taniqli
fan ventilyator
fan belt ventilyator qayishi
far uzoq; **How far is the next village?** Bundan keyingi qishloq uzoqmi?
fare: What is the fare? Qancha to'lash kerak?
farm ferma
farmer fermer; dehqon
farming dehqonchilik
Farsi forsi
fashion *couture* moda
fashion usul
fast *quick* tez
fasting: I am fasting. Ro'za tutyapman.

fat *adjective* semiz; **to get fat** semir-; *noun* yog'
father dada
faucet jo'mrak; kran
fax faks
fax machine faks apparati
fear *noun* qo'rqinch; *verb* qo'rq-
February fevral
federation federatsiya
feeding station ovqatlanish joyi
feel sez-
feeling his; tuyg'u
female *adjective* xotin; ayol; *animal* urg'ochi; *noun* xotin kishi
fence to'siq
fender qanot
ferret sassiq kuzan
ferry parom
fertile unumli
fertilizer o'g'it; dori
feud tortishuv
fever isitma
field dala
fifteen o'n besh
fifty ellik
fight janjal
fighter jangchi
file *paper* kartoteka; *computer* fayl
fill to'ldir-
fill in *a form* to'ldir-
film *movie* kino; *for camera* ply-onka
film-maker (kino-)rejissyor
filtered filtrlangan
filterless filtrsiz
final *adjective* oxirgi
final *noun* zachyot; imtihon
finance moliya
find top-
find out o'rgan-
fine *adjective* yaxshi (good); mayda (small); *adverb* yaxshi; *noun: of money* shtraf; jarima
finger barmoq

finish *verb* bitir-; tamom bo'l-
fire olov
firewood o'tin
first birinchi
first class birinchi klass/ sinf
fish baliq
fishing baliq ovlash
five besh
fix tuzat-
flash vspishka
flashlight qo'l fonari
flea burga
flee qoch-
flight *plane* reys
flight number reys nomeri
flint chaqmoq tosh
floating suvda qalqadigan; qalquvchan
flock *sheep* to'da; *birds* gala
flood sel
floor *ground* yer; *story* qavat; etaj
florist gulfurush
flour un
flower gul
flu gripp
flush: The toilet won't flush. Tualet ishlamayapti.
fly *noun* pashsha; *verb* uch-
fog tuman
foggy tuman tushgan
folk xalq
folk dancing xalq raqslari
folklore folklor
folk music xalq muzikasi
food ovqat
fool *noun* ahmoq; *verb* alda-
foot oyoq; *measurement* qadam
football futbol
foothills adirlar
footpath so'qmoq; yo'l
forbid man et-
forbidden man etilgan
foreign ajnabiy
foreigner chet ellik
forest o'rmon
forget esdan chiqar-

fork vilka
form *shape* shakl; *official* hujjat;
  verb yasa-; tashkil et-
fort qo'rg'on; qal'a
fortnight ikki hafta
forty qirq
forum forum
forward *adjective* oldingi; *verb*
  boshqasiga jo'nat-; o'tkaz-
forwards ilgari
found *verb* tashkil et-
foundation *organization* tashkilot
four to'rt
fourteen o'n to'rt
fourth to'rtinchi
fracture *noun* darz; *verb* darz ket-
franc frank
free ozod; **Is this seat free?** Bu
  joy bo'shmi?; **free of charge**
  bepul
freedom hurriyat
freeze muzla-
freight *noun* yuk; *verb* yuk
  yubor-
French *person* frantsuz; *language*
  frantsuzcha
french fries salomka
fresh yangi; *cool* salqin
Friday juma
fridge xolodilnik
friend o'rtoq
frighten qo'rqit-
frog qurbaqa
front *noun* old; **in front of** oldida
frontier chegara
frost qirov
frostbite sovuq oldirish
frostbitten hands/feet sovuq
  olgan qo'l/oyoq
fruit meva
fruit juice meva suvi; sok
fuel yonilg'i
fuel dump yonilg'i bazasi
full to'liq; **I am full!** To'yib ketdim.

full moon to'lin oy
funeral janoza
funny kulgili
furniture mebel'
future kelajak

G

gallon galon
game o'yin; match
gangrene gangrena
gangster mafioza
garage garaj
garden bog'cha
garbage musor; axlat
garlic sarimsoq piyoz; chisnok
garrison garnizon
gas gaz; *petrol* benzin
gas bottle gaz balloni
gas field gaz maydoni
gas production gaz ishlab
  chiqarish
gas well gaz qudug'i
gate darvoza
gear peredacha
general *adjective* umumiy; *noun*
  general
genitals jinsiy a'zolar
genocide genotsid
geologist geolog
Georgia Gruziya
Georgian gruzin; *language*
  gruzincha
German nemis; *language* nemischa
Germany Germaniya
germs mikroblar
get ol-
get up tur-
giant gigant
gift sovg'a; podarka
girl qiz bola
girlfriend yaxshi ko'radigan qiz
give ber-; **Give me ...** Menga
  ... bering.

give birth tug'-
glass *substance* oyna; *drinking* stakan; **a glass of water** bir stakan suv
glasses ko'zoynak
gloves qo'lqop
go bor-; yur-; **Go!** Yuring!; **Let's go!** Ketdik!
go out chiq-
go to bed yot-
goal *aim* maqsad; *soccer* gol
goat echki
God Xudo; Ollo
gold tilla; oltin
golf golf
good yaxshi
good bye! Xayr!
good luck! Sizga omad!
goose g'oz
government hukumat
grain g'alla
gram gramm
grammar grammatika
grandchild nevara
grandfather buva
grandmother buvi
grape uzum
grass o't
grateful: I am grateful. Minnatdorman.
grave *adjective* jiddiy; *noun* qabr
gravel shag'al
great ulug'; buyuk
greatest eng buyuk
Greek grek; *language* grek tili
green ko'k; yashil
greengrocer sabzavot do'koni
grenade granata
grind *grain* yanch-; *meat* qiymala-
ground meat qiyma
group gruppa
grow o's-
grow crops ekin ek-
grow up o's-; katta bo'l-
guard *noun* navbatchi; **border guard** chegarachi; *verb*
qo'riqla-
guerrilla partizan
guest mehmon
guesthouse mehmonxona
guest speaker mehmon notiq
guide *noun* gid; *verb* boshla-; yo'l ko'rsat-
guidebook ma'lumotnoma; spravochnik
gum; chewing gum saqich; zvochka
gun miltiq
gynecologist ginekolog
Gypsy: *Central Asian* lo'li; *European* tsigan

H

hair *on head* soch; *on body* tuk; qil
hairbrush soch cho'tkasi
haircut prichyoska; **I want a haircut please.** Sochimni kaltalatmoqchiman.
hairdresser ayollar sartaroshxonasi
hairdryer fen
half yarim
hamburger gamburger
hammer bolg'a
hand qo'l
handbag sumka
handicraft qo'lhunar
handle dastak; ruchka
hand over topshir-
handset trubka
hang os-
hangar angar
hangover *see* **headache**
happen bo'l-
happy xursand
harbor gavan
hard *not soft* qattiq; *difficult* qiyin
hardware store xo'jalik mollari do'koni
harmful zararli

harvest hosil
hat shapka
hate yomon ko'r-
have: I have two cars. Ikkita mashinam bor.; I don't have time. Vaqtim yo'q.
have to -ish kerak; I have to go. Ketishim kerak.
hay xashak
haystack g'aram
he u
head bosh; *boss/leader* boshliq
headache: I have a headache. Boshim og'riyapti.
head of state davlat boshlig'i
headquarters general shtab; qarorgoh
headscarf ro'mol
heal *by itself* tuzal-; *to treat* davola-; tuzat-
health sog'liq
healthcare sog'liq xizmati
healthy sog'
hear eshit-
heart yurak
heart attack infarkt
heart condition yomon yurak
heat *noun* issiqlik
heating otopleniye
heating coil kipyatilnik
heatwave juda issiq payt
heaven jannat
heavy og'ir
helicopter vertolyot
hell do'zax
hello! assalomu alaykum!; salom alaykum!; *to which the reply is* alaykum assalom *formal, or just* assalomu alaykum; *on the phone* alo!
help *noun* yordam; *verb* yordam ber-; Can you help me? Menga yordam berolasizmi?; help! dod!/yordam beringlar!
hen tovuq
hepatitis sariq
her u(ni)

herb o't
herd poda
here shu yerda
here is/are ... mana ...
hero qahramon
hers uniki
herself o'ziniki
hide bekitib qo'y-
high baland; high blood pressure yuksak qon bosimi; davlenie
hill tepa
him uni
himself o'zi
Hindu hindu
Hinduism hindu dini
hire ijaraga ol-
his uniki
historian tarixchi
history tarix
hit ur-; to hit a mine mina bos-
hold ushla-
hole teshik
holiday bayram
homeland vatan
homeless uysiz
honey asal
honeymoon asal oyi
hood of car kapot
hook qarmoq
horse ot
horse racing poyga
horse-riding ot minish
hose shlang
hospital bolnitsa; kasalxona
host uy egasi
hostage asir
hostel mehmonxona
hot issiq; *spicy* achchiq
hotel mehmonxona
hot water issiq suv
hour soat
house uy
housing estate/project kvartal
how? qanday?; qanaqa?; qanaqa qilib?; how are you? qalaysiz?; how far? necha kilo-

metr?; **how many?** Nechta?;
how much? Qancha?
however ammo
human *adjective* inson
human being inson
humanitarian beg'araz
humanitarian aid beg'araz
yordam
human rights inson huquqlari
humor yumor
humorous kulgili
hundred yuz
hungry: I'm hungry. Qornim
och.
hunt ovla-
hurry: I'm in a hurry. Shoshyapman.
hurt: Where does it hurt?
Qayeringiz og'riyapti?; **It hurts
here.** Shu yer og'riyapti.
husband er; xo'jayin
hygiene gigiena

I

I men
ice muz
ice cream morojniy; muz qaymoq
ice pick alpinistlar boltasi
I.D.: Do you have any I.D.?
Dokumentingiz bormi?
idea fikr
identification *see* I.D.
if -sa; **if possible** mumkin bo'lsa
ill: I am ill. Mazam yo'q.
illegal mumkin emas
illness kasallik
image rasm
imam imom
immigrant muhojir; immigrant
immigration muhojirlik; immigratsiya
import *verb* import qil-
importance ahamiyat

important muhim
impossible mumkin emas
improve yaxshilan-; yaxshi bo'l-
in -da; **in front of** oldida
included -ga kiradi
independence mustaqillik
independent mustaqil
independent state mustaqil
davlat
India Hinduston
Indian hind
indicator light indikator chirog'i
**indigestion: I have indiges-
tion.** Qornim og'riyapti.
industry sanoat
infant go'dak
infection yiring(lagan joy)
influenza gripp
information ma'lumot
information office ma'lumotlar byurosi
Ingush ingush
injure shikastla-; yarala-; lat ye-
injured shikastlangan; yaralangan
injury shikast; lat
ink siyoh
inner-tube ballon
innocent begunoh
inquiry surishtiruv
insane jinni; aqldan ozgan
inscription yozuv
insect hashorat
insecticide (hashorat tushiradigan) dori
instead o'rnida
institute institut
**insurance: I have medical
insurance.** Tibbiy sug'urtam
bor.
insurance policy sug'urta
**insured: My possessions are
insured.** Narsalarim sug'urta
qilingan.
intention niyat
**interested: to be interested
in** -ga qiziq-
interesting qiziq

interior ichki; ichkari
internal flight ichki reys
Internally Displaced Person
(o'z mamlakatining ichida) qochoq
international code xalqaro kod
international flight xalqaro reys
international operator xalqaro telegrafist
Internet internet
interpreter tarjumon
interval ora
interview interv'yu
into ichiga
introduce tanishtir-
introduction muqaddima
invasion bosqin
invention ixtiro (qilingan narsa)
inventor ixtirochi
investigate surishtir-
investigation surishtirish
invitation taklifnoma
invite taklif qil-; chaqir-
Iran Eron
Iranian eronlik
Ireland Irlandiya
Irish irlandiyalik
iron temir; *for clothes* dazmol
Islam Islom
Israel Isroil
it u
Italian italiyan; *language* italyancha
Italy Italya
itch qichi-
its uniki
itself o'zi

J

jack *car* domkrat
jacket kostyum
January yanvar
Japan Yaponiya
Japanese yapon; *language* yaponcha
jaw jag'
jazz jaz
jeans jinsi shim
Jew jugut
jewelry zirak-uzuk; zargarlik buyumlari
Jewish yahudiy
job ish
joke hazil; anekdot; **to joke** hazillash-; **it's no joke!** behazil!
journalist muxbir
Judaism yahudiy dini
judge sudya
July iyul
jumpstart: Can you jump-start the car? Mashinani itarishib yuborolasizmi?
June iyun
just faqatgina
justice adolat

K

Kabardian kabardiy
Kalmuk qalmoq
Karachai qorachoy
Kazakh qozoq
kebab shashlik; kabob
keep ob qo'y-
ketchup ketchup
kettle choygun
key kalit
kidnap (odam) o'g'irla-
kidnapper (odam) o'g'risi
kidney buyrak
kilim pallos
kill o'ldir-
killer qotil
kilogram kilo
kilometer kilometr
kind *adjective* yaxshi; muloyim; *noun* xil; **all kinds** har xil; **what kind?** qanaqa?

king podsho
kiosk kiosk
kiss o'p-
kitchen kuxnya
knee tizza
kneel cho'kka tush-
knife pichoq
knock taqillat-
know *something* bil-; *someone* tani-; **I know.** Bilaman.; **I don't know.** Bilmadim.; **Do you know him/her?** Uni taniysizmi?
knowledge bilim
known: ma'lum; well-known mashhur
kolkhoz kolxoz
Koran Qur'on
Kurd kurd

L

laboratory laboratoriya
ladder narvon
lake ko'l
lamb *animal* qo'zi; *meat* qo'y go'shti
lamp chiroq
land yer
landing strip uchish maydonchasi
landslide yer ko'chkisi
language til
lap qo'yin
laptop computer laptop kompyuter
large katta
larger kattaroq
last *adjective* oxirgi; *verb* chida-
late kech; to be late kech qol-
laugh *verb* kul-
laundry kir
laundry service kir yuvish xizmati
law qonun
law court sud
lawyer advokat

lay yotqiz-
lay mines mina joylashtir-
lazy dangasa
lead *noun* qo'rg'oshin
lead *verb* boshla-
leader rahbar
leaf barg
leak oq-
lean egil-
leap sakra-
learn o'rgan-
leather teri
leave ket-; chiqib ket-
lecture lektsiya
left chap
left-wing so'l; so'lchi
leg oyoq
legal qonuniy
legend afsona
lemon limon
lend qarzga ber-
lengthen cho'z-
lens linza; contact lenses kontakt linza
less kamroq
lesson dars
letter xat
lettuce salat
level *adjective* tekis; *noun* shayton
lever richag
liberation ozodlik
library kutubxona
lie *noun* yolg'on
lie down yot-
life hayot
lift *elevator* lift; *verb* ko'tar-
light *adjective: not dark* och rang; *not heavy* yengil; *noun: natural* yorug'; *electric* chiroq; **Do you have a light?** Gugurtingiz bormi?; *verb* yoq-; **May we light a fire?** O't yoqsak bo'ladimi?
light bulb lampochka
lighter chaqmoq; zajigalka
lighting chiroqlar

light meter yorug'lik o'lchaydigan apparat
lightning yashin
like *verb* I like ... Yaxshi ko'raman.; Menga yoqadi.; I don't like ... Yaxshi ko'rmayman.; Menga yoqmaydi.; *preposition* like that unaqa; ana shunga o'xshagan; like this bunaqa; mana bunga o'xshagan
likely bo'ladiganga o'xshaydi
limbs qo'l-oyoq
lime *fruit* limetta; *chemical* ohak
limit chet
line chiziq
linguist tilshunos
linguistics tilshunoslik
lip lab
lipstick pomada
list ro'yxat
listen eshit-
liter litr
literature adabiyot
little kichkina; a little bit ozgina
live *somewhere* tur-; *exist* yasha-
liver jigar
lizard kaltakesak
loaf bitta (buxonka non)
local mahalliy
location joy
lock qulf
locomotive parovoz
long uzun
look qara-
look for izla-; qidir-
loose change mayda pul
lose yo'qot-; I have lost my key. Kalitimni yo'qotib qo'ydim.; I am lost. Adashib qoldim.
lost *see* lose
lot/a lot ko'p
loud baland (ovoz)
loudly baland ovoz bilan
louse bit
love *noun* muhabbat; *verb* sev-
low past

low blood pressure gipotoniya
LP plastinka
luck: good luck! Sizga omad; muvaffaqiyat!
lunch *noun* obed; *verb* obed qil-
lung o'pka

M

machine mashina; apparat
machine gun avtomat
madrasa madrasa
mafia mafia
magazine jurnal
magnetic magnitli
magpie zag'izxon
mail pochta
mailbox pochta yashigi
main asosiy; bosh
main square skver; maydon
maintain saqla-
maize makka jo'xori
majority ko'pchilik
make qil-
make-up pomada
male erkak
mammal sutemizuvchi
man erkak kishi
manager menejer; direktor
manual book qo'llanma
manual worker ishchi
many ko'p; too many juda ko'p; how many? Nechta?
map xarita; karta; map of Tashkent Toshkent xaritasi
March mart
mare baytal
marital status madaniy hol
mark belgi
market bozor
marriage er-xotinlik
married: I am married. *said by a man* Uylanganman.; *said by a woman* Turmushqa chiqqanman.

marsh botqoq
martyr shahid; qurbon
mascara surma
massacre qatli om
match *soccer* futbol matchi
matches gugurt
material material; *cloth* mato
mathematics matematika
matter: It doesn't matter.
Hechqisi yo'q.
mattress matras
mausoleum maqbara
May may
may: May I? Mumkinmi?
maybe mumkin; balki
me meni; mendan; menga
meal ovqat; ovqatlanish payti
mean *verb* de-; **What does this
mean?** Bu nima degani?;
What do you mean? Nima
demoqchisiz?
meaning ma'no
measure *verb* o'lcha-
meat go'sht
mechanic mexanik
media axborot vositalari
medical tibbiy
medical insurance tibbiy
sug'urta
medication dori
medicine dori
meet uchrash-
meeting majlis; uchrashuv
melon qovun
member a'zo
memory xotira
menthol yalpizli
menu menyu
mercenary yollanma askar
message xat
metal metal; temir
meter metr
metro metro
microscope mikroskop
middle o'rta
middle name ota ismi
midnight yarim kecha

midsummer yoz chillasi
midwife enaga
midwinter qish chillasi
mild winter unchalik sovuq
bo'lmagan qish
mile mil
military harbiy
milk sut
mill tegirmon
millet tariq
million million
minaret minora
mine *adjective* meniki; *noun:
excavation* kon; *explosive* mina
mine detector mina detektori
mine disposal minalarni
zararsizlantirish
minefield minalashtirilgan joy
miner konchi
mineral mineral
mineral water gazli suv
minister vazir
ministry vazirlik
Ministry of Agriculture Qishloq
Xo'jaligi Vazirligi
Ministry of Defense Mudofaa
Vazirligi
Ministry of Education Xalq
Ta'limi Vazirligi
Ministry of Foreign Affairs
Tashqi Ishlar Vazirligi
Ministry of Health Sog'liqni
Saqlash Vazirligi
Ministry of Internal Affairs
Ichki Ishlar Vazirligi
Ministry of Justice Adliya
Vazirligi
minority *group* mayda millat;
minority vote kamchilik
ovoz
minute *noun* minut
miracle mo'jiza
mirror oyna
missile raketa
mist tuman
mistake xato; **to make a mis-
take** xato qil-

misty tumanli
misunderstand noto'g'ri tushun-
mobile phone uyali/sotoviy telefon
model model
modem modem
modern zamonaviy
moment lahza; Wait a moment! Birpas turib turing!
monarch podshoh
Monday dushanba
money pul
monk rohib
month oy
monument yodgorlik
moon oy; **full moon** to'lin oy; **new moon** yangi oy
more ...dan ko'p; ko'proq
more or less taxminan
morning ertalab; **this morning** bugun ertalab
mosque machit
mosquito chivin
most ko'p
mother ona; oyi
motorbike mototsikl
mountain tog'
mountain pass dovon; pereval
mouse sichqon
mouth og'iz
mouthwash og'iz chayish uchun suv
move qimirla-; *house* ko'ch-
movie kino
much ko'p; **not much** ozgina; **too much** juda ko'p; **how much?** qancha?; **how much is it?** qancha turadi?
mud loy
mulberry tut
mule xachir
mullah mullo
murder *noun* qotillik; *verb* o'ldir-
murderer qotil
museum muzey

music muzika
Muslim muslim
must -ish kerak; **I must see it.** Ko'rishim kerak.
mustache mo'ylov
mustard gorchitsa
my mening
myself o'zim

N

Nagorno-Karabakh Tog'li Qorabog'
nail mix; **finger nail** tirnoq
nail-clippers tirnoq oladigan
Nakhichevan Naxichevan
name ism; ot; **surname** familiya; **What is your name?** Ismingiz?/Otingiz nima?; **My name is Fred.** Ismim Fred.
napkin salfetka
narrow tor
nation *state* davlat; *people* millat
nationality millat; *& see* **citizenship**
natural tabiiy
natural disaster tabiiy ofat
natural resources tabiiy boylik
nature tabiat
navy dengiz floti
near -ga yaqin
nearby yaqin
necessary: It's necessary. Kerak.
neck bo'yin
necklace munchoq
necktie galstuk
need kerak; **I need ...** Menga ... kerak.
needle igna
negotiator muzokara olib boruvchi
neighbor qo'shni
neither ... nor na ... na ... emas

nerve asab; **It's getting on my nerves.** Asabimga tegdi.
net to'r
neutral drive neytral
never hech qachon
new yangi
news xabarlar; axborot
news agency axborot agenti
newspaper gazeta; **newspaper in English** inglizcha gazeta
newsstand kiosk
New Year *March 21* Navruz; *January 1* Yangi Yil
New Zealand Yangizilandiya
next keyingi; **next week** keyingi hafta
nice yaxshi
night kecha; **good night!** yaxshi dam oling(lar)!
nightclub klub
nine to'qqiz
nineteen o'n to'qqiz
ninety to'qson
no yo'q; **no entry** kirish mumkin emas; **no smoking** chekish mumkin emas; **no sugar, please** rahmat, shakar olmayman
nobody hech kim
Nogai no'g'ay
noise tovush
noisy shovqin
noon tush vaqti; obed
no one hech kim
nor: neither ... nor na ... na ... emas.
normal oddiy
north *noun* shimol
north(ern) shimoliy
Northern Ireland Shimoliy Irlandiya
nose burun
not emas; **This isn't good.** Bu yaxshi emas.; **do not ... !** ...-ma!
not enough yetarli emas

note: bank note banknot
notebook daftar
nothing hech nima
nought nul
noun ism
novel roman; **novels in English** inglizcha romanlar
November noyabr
now hozir
nowhere hech qayer
nuclear power yadro energiyasi; *political state* yadro quroliga ega davlat
nuclear power station yadro stantsiyasi
number nomer
nun rohiba
nurse hamshira

oak eman
obligation majburiyat
observer kuzatuvchi
occasion fursat
occupation *job* kasb
occupation *of a country* ishg'ol
occupying forces ishg'ol qiluvchilar; bosqinchilar
occur bo'l-
o'clock: It is ... o'clock. Soat ... bo'ldi.
October oktyabr
of course albatta
office idora
officer *military* ofitser
office worker xodim
offshore qirg'ogdan narida
often ko'p
oil neft; *cooking* yog'
oilcan yog' bankasi
oilfield neft maydoni
oil pipeline neft kamari
oil production neft ishlab-chiqarish

oil refinery neftni aralash-malardan tozalovchi zavod
oil slick suvning ustida yoyilgan neft
oil spill neft to'kilishi
oil tanker neft tankeri
oil well neft qudug'i
oil worker neftchi
old: *things* eski; *people* qari; **How old are you?** Yoshingiz nechada?; **I am ... years old.** ... yoshdaman.
Old City Eski Shahar
on ustida; -da; **on time** vaqtida
once bir marta
one bir
one-way street bir tomonlama yo'l
one-way ticket borish bileti
onion piyoz
only faqat
onto ustiga
open *adjective* ochiq; *verb* och-
opera opera
opera house opera zali
operating theater operatsiya xonasi
operation *surgical* operatsiya
operator; telephone operator telegrafist
opposite *noun* teskarisi; *preposition* ro'parasida
opposition oppozitsiya
or yoki
orange *fruit* apelsin; *color* to'q sariq
order *noun* buyruq; *verb:* *someone* buyur-; *food* **I'd like to order ...** ... olaman.
ordinary oddiy
origin kelib chiqish; asl
original dastlabki; asliy
orphan yetim
Orthodox pravoslav
other boshqa
ounce unts
our bizning; **ours** bizniki

ourselves o'zimiz
out: **He went out.** Chiqib ketdi.; **He threw it out.** Tashlab ketdi.; **The lights went out.** Svet o'chdi.
outside *adjective* ko'chadagi; **He went outside.** Ko'chaga chiqdi.
overcoat pal'to
overtake o'zib ket-; o'tib ket-
owl boyo'g'li
own *adjective* o'z; *verb:* **I own a house.** Uyim bor.; **They own two cars.** Ularning ikkita mashinasi bor.
oxygen kislorod

P

package posilka
padlock qulf
pain og'riq
painkiller og'riq qoldiruvchi dori
paint *noun* bo'yoq; *verb* bo'ya-
painter rassom
painting rasm
Pakistan Pokiston
Pakistani pokistonlik
palace saroy
pale rangi so'lgan
paper *substance* qog'oz; *newspaper* gazeta; *article* maqola; ocherk; **a piece of paper** bir varaq qog'oz
parachute parashyut
paradise jannat
paralyze shol qil-
parcel posilka
parents ota-ona
park *noun* park; bog'; **to park a car** mashinani qo'y-
parliament parlament; *Uzbek* Oliy Majlis
part qism

participate ishtirok et-; qatna-
partridge kaklik
party o'tirish; *political* partiya
pass o't-; *& see* **mountain pass**
passable: Is the road passable? Bu yo'ldan yursa bo'ladimi?
passenger yo'lovchi
passport pasport
passport number pasport nomeri
past *adjective* o'tgan; *noun* o'tgan zamon
pasta makaron
path yo'l
patient *medical* kasal
pay *noun* oylik; *verb* to'la-
payment haq
peace tinchlik
peace-keeping troops tinchlik saqlovchi qo'shinlar
peace talks tinchlik muzokaralari
peach shaftoli
peak cho'qqi
pear nok
pearl dur
peasant dehqon
pediatrician pediatr
pediatrics pediatriya
pelvis tos suyagi
pen ruchka
pencil qalam
penicillin penitsillin
penknife pakki
people odamlar
pepper: *red* garmdori; *black* qora murch
perfect nuqsonsiz
perform *role* o'yna-; *duty* bajar-
performance o'yin
perfume atir
perhaps balki
period muddat
Persian *person* fors
persimmon xurmo
person odam; kishi
petrol benzin

petroleum neft
pharmacy apteka
phone *noun* telefon; *verb* telefon qil-
phonetics fonetika
photo rasm
photocopier kseroks mashinasi
photocopy kseroks
photographer fotograf
photography fotografiya
physics fizika
physiotherapy fizioterapiya
piano pianino
pickax qo'shbosh
picture rasm; surat
pig cho'chqa
pigeon kaptar
pilau palov; osh
pilgrim ziyoratchi
pilgrim *to Mecca* hoji
pill tabletka
pillow yostiq
pilot pilot
pin igna
pine qarag'ay
pink pushti
pins and needles: to have pins and needles uvishib qol-
pipe trubka
pistachio pista
piste chang'i yo'li
pistol to'pponcha
pitch yelim
pizza pitsa
place joy; yer
place of birth tug'ilgan joy
plain *noun* dala
plane samolyot; *tree* chinor
plank taxta
plant o'simlik
planting ekish
plastic plastmassa
plate tarelka
platform platforma; *station* perron
platform number perron nomeri
play *theater* o'yin; *verb* o'yna-; *a musical instrument* chal-

please! iltimos!
pleasure kayf
plow *noun* plug; *verb* yer hayda-
plug *bath* probka; *electric* shtepsel vilkasi
plum olxo'ri; **sour plum** ko'k sulton
p.m. tushdan keyin
pocket cho'ntak
podium minbar
poem she'r
poet shoir
poison zahar
police militsiya
policeman militsioner
police station militsiya uchastkasi
polite odobli; tarbiyali
political siyosiy
political scientist siyosat-shunos
politician siyosatchi
politics siyosat
pollution (atrof-muhit) ifloslanishi
pomegranate anor
pony toychoq
pool basseyn
poor kambag'al
poplar terak
population aholi
pork cho'chqa g'oshti
port port
portable TV ko'tarib yuradigan televizor
portion *food* portsiya; *share* ulush
portrait surat
position pozitsiya; joy
possible mumkin; **if possible** mumkin bo'lsa
postcard otkritka
post office pochta
potato kartoshka
pottery sopol idishlar
pound funt
pour quy-
pour out to'k-

P.O.W. asir
P.O.W. camp asirlar lageri
powder poroshok
power quvvat
praise maqta-
pray: *private* duo qil-; *Muslim daily prayers* namoz o'qi-
prayer rug joynamoz
prefer yaxshiroq ko'r-
pregnant homilador; **I'm pregnant.** Homiladorman.
premier prem'yer
prepare tayyorla-
present *adjective* hozirgi; *time* hozirgi zamon; *gift* sovg'a
president prezident
press: the press matbuot
pressure bosim; **high blood pressure** gipotoniya; **low blood pressure** gipertoniya
previously oldin
price narx
pride g'urur
priest po'p
prime minister bosh vazir
principle qoida; printsip
print bos-
printer *computer* printer
prison qamoq
prisoner asir; tutqun
prize mukofot
probable ehtimol; **it is probable** bo'lsa kerak.
probably: We'll probably go. Borsak kerak.
problem problema; masala; **no problem!** Xo'p!/Hechqisi yo'q.
product mahsulot
profession kasb
professional professional
professor professor
program programma; **radio program** radio programmasi
projector proyektor
pronounce talaffuz qil-
pronunciation talaffuz

proof isbot
prosthesis protez
protect qo'riqla-; himoya qil-
protection himoya
protest *noun* protest; *verb* namoyish qil-
proud mag'rur
prove isbotla-
proverb masal
pub pivoxona
public phone telefon-avtomat
publish nashr qil-
publisher nashriyot
pull tort-
pump *noun* nasos; *verb* nasos bilan tort-; quy-
pumping station nasos stantsiyasi
pumpkin osh qovoq
puncture teshik; **I have a puncture.** Ballon teshilgan.
punish jazola-
pupil o'quvchi
purple siyoh rang
push itar-
put qo'y-
put on clothes kiyin-
put through *on the phone* ulab ber-

Q

quarter: *area* kvartal; **one-quarter** to'rtdan bir; **three-quarters** to'rtdan uch
queen xotin podsho
question savol
quick tez
quickly tez
quiet *adjective* tinch
quietly sekin
quilt ko'rpa(cha)
quit tashla-; tashlab ket-
Qur'an Qur'on

R

rabbit quyon
rabies quturish
radar radar
radiator radiator
radio radio
radio broadcast radio eshittirishi
radio program radio programmasi
radio station radio stantsiyasi
radio taxi radioli taksi
raid bos-
railway temir yo'l
railway station vokzal
rain yomg'ir
rainbow kamalak
rain: it is raining yomg'ir yog'yapti
rainy weather yog'ingarchilik
raise ko'tar-
ram qo'chqor
Ramadan ramazon
range plita
rape zo'rla-; nomusga teg-; **I've been raped.** Meni bittasi zo'rladi.
rapid tez
rapidly tez
rat kalamush
rate: What is the exchange rate? Kurs qancha?
ravage *verb* vayron qil-
ravine soy
raw xom
razor britva
razorblade lezvie
reactionary reaktsioner
read o'qi-
ready tayyor; **I am ready.** Tayyorman.
real haqiqiy; chin
reality haqiqat
realize: I didn't realize any-

thing was wrong. Hech nima payqamadim.

reaping o'rish

reason sabab; for that reason -dan tufayli; shu sababdan

reason for travel sayohat qil-ishdan maqsad

rebel *noun* isyonchi

receipt kvitantsiya

receive ol-; qabul qil-

recently yaqinda

reception desk registratsiya

recognize tani-

record *noun* plastinka; *sports* rekord; *document* hujjat; *verb* yoz-

red qizil

Red Cross Qizil Xoch

referee sudya; hakam

refine aralashmalardan tozala-

refinery aralashmalardan tozalovchi zavod; **oil refinery** neftni aralashmalardan tozalovchi zavod

refrigerator xolodilnik

refugee qochoq; *plural* qochoqlar

refugee camp qochoqlar lageri

regime rejim

region rayon; mintaqa

registered mail zakaz xat

reign *noun* hukmronlik; davr

relationship aloqa

relative qarindosh; *plural* qarindoshlar

relax dam ol-

release qo'yib yubor-

relief aid yordam

religion din

remain qol-

remember esla-

repair *noun* remont; *verb* tuzat-; remont qil-

reparation jarima

repeat qaytar-

replace almashtir-

reply javob ber-

report maqola; reportaj

represent vakil bo'l-

representation vakillik

representative vakil

republic jumhuriyat; respublika

research tadqiqot

reservation: bron; I have a reservation. Joyni bronlaganman.

reserve bronla-; Can I reserve a place? Joy bronlasam bo'ladimi?

reserved bronlangan

reserves zapas

rest *relaxation* dam olish; *others* boshqalar; qolganlar; *verb* dam ol-

restaurant oshxona; restoran

return qayt-

return ticket borish-kelish bileti

reverse *adjective* teskari; orqa; *verb* boshga ol-

review *newspaper* taqriz; retsenziya

revolution inqilob

rice *uncooked* guruch; *cooked* palov

rich boy

ride *a horse* min-

rifle miltiq

right *correct* to'g'ri; You are right. Gapingiz to'g'ri.; **right side** o'ng tomon

rights huquqlar; **civil rights** fuqaro huquqlari; **human rights** inson huquqlari

right-wing o'ngchilar

ring *noun* uzuk; *verb* telefon qil-; I want to call ... -ga telefon qilmoqchiman

riot to'polon

ripe pishgan

rise tur-; ko'taril-

risk xavflilik

river daryo

river bank qirg'oq

road yo'l

roadblock post
road map yo'l xaritasi
rob so'y-; **I've been robbed.** Narsalarimni o'g'irlashdi.
robbery o'g'irlash
rock tosh
rock concert rok-n-rol kontserti
rock 'n' roll rok muzikasi
roof tom
room xona; **single room** bir kishilik xona; **double room** ikki kishilik xona
room number xona nomeri
room service tozalash xizmati
rooster xo'roz
rope arqon
rosary tasbeh
rose atirgul
route yo'l; marshrut
row *line* saf
royal podshoga oid
rubber kauchuk
rubbish axlat
ruble rubl; so'm
rude adabsiz
rug gilam
rugby regbi
ruins xaroba
ruler *person* hokim; *for measuring* lineyka
run chop-
run out tamom bo'l-; tuga-; **I have run out of gas.** Benzin tugadi.
Russia Rossiya
Russian rus; *language* ruscha
rust zang

S

sack qop
sad xafa
safe *adjective* xavfsiz; *noun* seyf
safety xavfsizlik
safety pin to'g'nog'ich

saffron za'faron
saint avliyo
saint's tomb ziyoratgoh
salad salat
salesperson sotuvchi
salon *shop* do'kon
salt tuz
salty sho'r
samovar samovar
sand qum
sandwich buterbrot
satellite sputnik
satellite phone sputnik telefoni
satisfactory yetarli; qanoatli
satisfied mamnun
Saturday shanba kuni
sausage sosiska; **horse sausage** qazi
save *rescue* qutqar-; *money* teja-
saw *noun* arra
say ayt-
scarf sharf
scatter tarqal-
school maktab
science ilm
scientific ilmiy
scientist olim
scissors qaychi
score: What's the score? Hisob necha bo'ldi?; **Who scored?** Kim gol urdi?
Scot shotlandiyalik
Scotland Shotlandiya
Scottish shotlandiyalik
screw vint
screwdriver otvertka
scythe chalg'i o'roq
sea dengiz
search izla-
season fasl
seat o'rindiq; joy; *political* o'rin
second *adjective* ikkinchi; *noun* sekund
second class ikkinchi klas
second-hand ishlatilgan
secret *adjective* maxfiy; *noun* sir
secretary sekretar; kotib

secret police S.N.B.
section qism; bo'lim
security xavfsizlik
see ko'r-
seed urug'
seek izla-
seismic survey seysmologik tadqiqot
seize tortib ol-
sell sot-
send yubor-
senior katta
sense tuyg'u
September sentyabr
septic septik
series seriya
serious jiddiy
service xizmat
session sessiya
seven yetti
seventeen o'n yetti
seventy yetmish
several bir necha
severe winter qattiq qish
sew tik-
sex jins; *sexual relations* jinsiy aloqa
shade soya
shah shoh
shake chayqat-
shampoo shampun
shape shakl
share *verb* bo'lish-
sharp o'tkir
shaving cream soqol olish uchun krem
she u
sheep qo'y
sheepdog cho'pon iti
sheet choyshab
shell *of nut* qobiq
shell *military* snaryad
shelter panoh
shepherd cho'pon
shine porla-
ship kema
shirt ko'ylak

shock *medical* shok
shoes tufli
shoeshop poyafzal do'koni
shoot ot-; don't shoot! otmang!
shop do'kon
shopkeeper do'kondor
shopping bozor qil- (to go …)
shore yoqa
short kalta
shortage defitsit
shoulder yelka
shout baqir-
shovel belkurak
show *noun* ko'rgazma; programma; *verb* ko'rsat-
shower dush
shrapnel snaryad parchasi
shrine ziyoratgoh
shut *adjective* yopiq; *verb* yop-
Siberia Sibir
sick kasal; I am sick. Kasalman.
sidestreet tor ko'cha
sight tomosha qilinadigan joy
sign *noun* belgi; yozuv
sign an agreement shartnomaga qo'l qo'y-
sign language imo-ishora tili
signature imzo
significance ahamiyat
significant ahamiyatli
silence jimjitlik
silent jimjit
silk ipak
silly bachkana
silver kumush
similar shuningdek; shunaqa
since …dan beri
sing ashula ayt-
single bitta; single room bir kishilik xona; I am single. *said by a man* Bo'ydoqman.; *said by a woman* Turmushqa chiqmaganman.
sink *noun* umivalnik; *verb* bot-
sister: *younger* singil; *older* opa
sit o'tir-

situation vaziyat
six olti
sixteen o'n olti
sixth oltinchi
sixty oltmish
size kattalik; razmer
skating konki uchish
skiing chang'i uchish
skill mohirlik
skilled mohir; epchil
skin teri
ski slope chang'i uchadigan joy
sky osmon
sleep *noun* uyqi; *verb* uxla-
sleeping bag spal'niy meshok
sleeping car yotoq vagon
sleeping pill(s) uyqi dori
sleepy: I am sleepy. Uyqim
  kelyapti.
sleet do'l
sling *medical* bog'ich
slip kombinatsiya
slope qiyalik
slow sekin
slowly sekin
small kichkina
smaller kichkinaroq
smell *noun* hid
smoke *noun* tutun; *verb* chek-
smoking chekish
smuggler kontrabandist
snail shilliq qurt
snake ilon
snake bite ilon chaqishi
snow qor; It is snowing. Qor
  yog'yapti.
snowdrift qor uyumi
so shunaqangi
so much/many shuncha ko'p
soap sovun
soccer futbol
soccer match futbol matchi
social ijtimoiy
socialism sotsializm
socialist sotsialist
society jamiyat
sock noski

soft yumshoq
soldier soldat; askar
solstice quyosh turishi
solve hal qil-
some bir necha; ba'zi
somehow bir amallab
someone/somebody bittasi
something bir narsa; bir nima
sometimes ba'zan
somewhere bir joyda
son o'g'il
song ashula
soon yaqinda
sore throat tomoq og'rig'i
sorry! kechirasiz!; I'm sorry. Uzr.
soul jon
sound tovush
sound equipment zvukoap-
  paratura
soup sho'rva
sour nordon
source manba
sour plum ko'k sulton
south *noun* janub
south(ern) janubiy
souvenir yodgor
soviet sovet
Soviet Union Sovet Ittifoqi
sow ek-
spa kurort
space oraliq
spade kurak
Spanish ispaniyalik; *language*
  ispancha
spanner gayka klyuchi
spare tire zapas shina
sparkling drink gazli
speak: gapir-; Do you speak
  English? Inglizcha bilasizmi?;
  I speak ... ... gapiraman.
speaker *person* notiq; *parliament* notiq; *hi-fi* karnay
specialist mutaxassis
speed tezlik
spell: How do you spell that?
  Qanaqa yoziladi?
spend sarfla-

spicy *hot* achchiq
spider o'rgimchak
spill to'k-
spin aylan-
spine *of back* umurtqa
spit tufla-
splint *medical* taxtakach
split yor-
spoil buz-
sponge gubka
spoon qoshiq
sports sport
sportsman sportchi
spread yoy-
spring *season* bahor; *water* buloq; *metal* prujina
spy razvedka; shpion
square; town square skver
stadium stadion
staff xodimlar; shtab
stage sahna
stale suvi qochgan
stallion ayg'ir
stamp *postal* marka; *official* tamg'a; pechat'
stand tur-
star yulduz
state *nation* davlat; *in federation* shtat; *condition* ahvol
station stantsiya
stationer's kantselyariya do'koni
stationery kantselyariya jihozlari
statue haykal
stay: *in one place* tur-; *behind* qol-
steak bifshteks
steal o'g'irla-
steal: My ... has been stolen. ...-imni o'g'irlatdim.
steel po'lat
steering wheel rul
sterling sterling
stethoscope stetoskop
stick *noun* cho'p; kaltak; *verb* yopish-
still *adverb* hali ham
sting *verb* chaq-

stink *verb* sasi-
stitches *surgical* tikish
stolen o'g'irlangan
stomach qorin
stomachache: I have a stomachache. Qornim og'riyapti.
stone tosh
stop to'xta-; **don't stop!** to'xtamang!
store magazin; *shop* do'kon
stork laylak
storm bo'ron
story *report/tale* hikoya; *floor* etaj; qavat
stove plita
straight tekis; **straight on** to'g'riga; **Go straight ahead.** To'g'riga yuring.
strange g'alati
stranger begona
strawberry qulupnay
stream daryocha
street ko'cha
strength kuch
stretcher zambil
strike *from work* zabastovka
strike *verb: from work* zabastovka qil-
string ip
strong kuchli
structure tuzum
struggle kurash-
stuck: Our car is stuck. Mashinamiz yerga botib qoldi.
student o'quvchi; student
study *noun* tadqiqot; *verb* o'qi-; o'rgan-
subject mavzu
submachine gun avtomat
suburb shaharning atrofi
subway *metro* metro
success muvaffaqiyat
such shunaqa
suddenly birdan
sufficient yetarli
sugar shakar; *cube sugar* qand; *crystal sugar* novvot

suit kostyum-shim
suitable mos
suitcase chamadon
sultan sulton
summer yoz
summit cho'qqi
summit conference yuqori darajadagi uchrashuv
sun quyosh
sunblock cream quyoshdan saqlanish uchun krem
Sunday yakshanba; bozor kuni
sunflower seeds semyachka
sunglasses qora ko'zoynak
sunny quyoshli
sunny: It is sunny. Quyosh chiqdi.
sunrise kun chiqish payti
sunscreen *see* sunblock
sunset kunbotar vaqti
sunshine oftob
supermarket supermarket
supper (kechki) ovqat
supply *noun* zapas
surgeon xirurg; jarroh
surgery *operation* operatsiya
surname familiya
surprising ajoyib
swallow *bird* qaldirg'och; *verb* yut-
swamp botqoq
swear *an oath* qasam ich-; *curse* so'kin-
sweat *noun* ter; *verb* terla-
sweater jemper
sweep supur-
sweet shirin
sweet pepper qalampir; bulg'arskiy
swell shish-
swim suz-
swimming suzish
swimming pool basseyn
swing arg'imchoq
switch *electric* viklyuchatel
switch off o'chir-
switch on yoq-

sycamore *see* plane tree
symbol belgi
symphony simfoniya
symptom belgi; alomat
synagogue senago'g
syntax sintaksis
syringe shprits
system sistema

T

table stol
tablecloth dasturxon
tablet tabletka
Tajik tojik
take ol-
take off: What time does the plane take off? Samolyot qachon uchadi?
talk gapir-
tall baland bo'yli
tampon tampon
tandoor oven tandir
tank bak; *military* tank
tap *faucet* jo'mrak
tape kasseta
tape recorder magnitofon
taste *noun* ta'm; *verb* tot-
tasteless mazasiz
tasty shirin
tax *noun* soliq; *verb* soliq ol-
tax-free soliqsiz
tax-free zone soliqsiz zona
taxi taksi
tea choy; *green* ko'k choy; *black* pamil choy; **tea with milk** shirchoy
teach o'rgat-; o'qit-
teacher o'qituvchi
teacup *Uzbek* piyola
team kommanda
tear *noun* yirtiq joy
tear *verb* yirt-
tear gas yoshlantiruvchi gaz
teaspoon choy qoshig'i

time

technique uslub
teeth tish
telecommunications telealoqalar
telegram telegramma
telephone *noun* telefon; satellite phone sputnik telefoni;
verb telefon qil-
telephone center telemarkaz
telephone operator telegrafist
telephone station telefon
stantsiyasi
telescope durbin
television televizor
television station televidenie
stantsiyasi
telex teleks
tell ayt-; tell him/her unga ayting; tell me menga ayting
temperature temperatura; I
have a temperature. Isitmam
bor.
temple ibodatxona
ten o'n
tennis tennis
tent chodir
tent pegs qoziq
tenth o'ninchi
termite termit
terrible dahshatli
territory territoriya
test *noun* imtihon
text tekst
than: bigger than -dan katta;
smaller than -dan kichkina
thank rahmat de-
thank you! rahmat!
that ana u; o'sha
that's enough! Bo'ldi!
thaw *noun* qor erishi; *verb* eri-
theater teatr
theft o'g'rilik
their ularning
theirs ularniki
themselves ularning o'zi
then keyin
theory nazariya

there o'sha yerda; there is/are
bor; there is/are not yo'q
therefore shuning uchun
thermometer termometr
these bular
they ular
thick *wide* keng; *dense* quyuq
thief o'g'ri
thin: *thing* ingichka; *person*
ozg'in
thing narsa
think o'yla-; I think ... ... deb
o'ylayman
third *adjective* uchinchi; one-
third uchdan bir
thirsty: I'm thirsty. Chanqab
ketdim.
thirteen o'n uch
thirty o'ttiz
this mana bu
those o'sha
thought fikr
thousand ming
thread ip
three uch
three times uch marta
throat tomoq
thrombosis tromboz
throne taxt
through -dan; orqali
throw ot-
thumb bosh barmoq
thunder gumburlash
Thursday payshanba
tick *insect* kana
ticket bilet; one-way ticket
borish bileti; return ticket
borish-kelish bileti
ticket office kassa
tie *necktie* galstuk
tie *verb* bog'la-
ties: diplomatic ties diplomatik aloqalar
tights kolgotka
time vaqt; two times ikki
marta; for a long time
anchadan beri; free time

Uzbek Dictionary & Phrasebook · 91

bo'sh vaqt; **What time is it?** Soat necha bo'ldi?

timetable jadval

tire *noun* shina; *verb* charcha-

tired charchagan

tissues salfetka

transfer *on the phone* ula-

toast *drink* tost

tobacco tamaki; chewing tobacco nosvoy

today bugun

toe oyoq barmog'i

together birga

toilet tualet

toilet paper xo'jalik qog'ozi

toilet(s) tualet(lar)

token *coin* jeton

tomato pomidor

tomb maqbara

tomorrow ertaga; **the day after tomorrow** indinga

tongue til

tonight bugun kechasi

too *also* ham; *very* juda; **too little** juda kam; **too many/much** juda ko'p

tools asboblar

tooth tish

toothache tish og'rig'i

toothbrush tish cho'tkasi

toothpaste tish pastasi

toothpick tish kavlagich

top ust; tepa; **on top of** tepasida

torture *noun* qiynoq; *verb* qiynoqla-

tourism turizm

tourist sayohatchi; turist

tourist office turizm idorasi

tourniquet turniket

tow: Can you tow us? Bizni tortib ketolasizmi?

tow rope tros

towel sochiq

tower minora

town posyolka

town center tsentr; markaz

town hall gorispolkom

track reyls

tractor traktor

trade union kasaba uyushmasi; profsoyuz

tradition urf-odat

traditional milliy; an'anaviy

traffic lights svetofor

traffic police GAI

train poezd

train station vokzal

tranquilizer tinchlantiruvchi

transformer transformator

transfusion: blood transfusion qon quyish

translate tarjima qil-

translation tarjima

translator tarjumon

transmit yubor-; yo'nat-; yuqtir-

transmitter peredatchik

transport tashi-

trap qopqon

trash axlat; musor

trauma travma

travel *noun* sayohat; *verb* sayohat qil-

travel agent sayohat agentligi

traveler sayohatchi; yo'lovchi

traveler's checks sayohat cheklari

treacherous xavf-xatarli

treasury xazina

tree daraxt

trial *legal* sud; muhokama

trolley bus trolleybus

troops qo'shinlar; otryadlar

trouble: What's the trouble? Nima bo'ldi?

trousers shim

truce sulh

truck gruzovoy mashina

true to'g'ri; rost

trunk *of car* bagaj joyi

truth haqiqat

try *make effort* harakat qil-

tsar tsar

tube quvur; truba

Tuesday seshanba

tunnel tunel
turban salla
Turk turk
turkey induk
Turkey Turkiya
Turkish turkcha
Turkish baths hammom
turn buril-; **turn left!** Chapga buriling!; **turn right!** O'ngga buriling!
twelve o'n ikki
twenty yigirma
twice ikki marta
twins egizak
two ikki
two-thirds uchdan ikki
type *noun* tur; xil
typewriter mashinka
tyre *noun* shina

UFO uchar likopcha
Ukraine Ukraina
Ukrainian language ukraincha
ulcer yara; **stomach ulcer** oshqozon yarasi
umbrella zontik
uncle: *maternal* tog'a; *paternal* amaki
under ... ... tagida
underground yer tagida; *railway* metro
understand tushun-; **I understand.** Tushunaman.; **I don't understand.** Tushunmadim.
undertake kirish-
underwear ishton
undo yech-
UNDP Birlashgan Millatlar Taraqqiyot Programmasi
unemployed ishsiz
unemployment ishsizlik
UNESCO Birlashgan Millatlar Maorif, Ilm, va Madaniyat Tashkiloti
unexpected kutilmagan
unexploded bomb portlamagan bomba
unfortunate afsus
unfortunately afsuski
unhappy xafa
UNHCR Birlashgan Millatlar Qochoqlar uchun Oliy Komissari
unification birlashish
uniform forma
union ittifoq; **trade union** kasaba uyushmasi; profsoyuz
unique yagona; o'ziga xos
unite birlash-
united birlashgan
United Nations Birlashgan Millatlar Tashkiloti
university universitet
unknown noma'lum
until ... ...-gacha
up yuqoriga; tepaga
U.S.A. AQSh (Amerika Qo'shma Shtatlari)
use ishlat-; foydalan-
useful foydali
usual oddiy
usually odatda
Uzbek o'zbek; *language* o'zbekcha
Uzbekistan O'zbekiston

vacation kanikul; dam olish payti
vaccinated: I have been vaccinated. Emlanganman.
valley vodiy
van furgon
variety har xillik
varnish lak
vase vaza
vegetables sabzavot

vegetable shop sabzavot do'koni
vegetarian: I am a vegetarian. Vegeterianman.
vein qon tomiri
venereal disease tanosil kasalligi
verb fe'l
very juda
veto veto
vice-president vitse prezident; prezident muovini
victim qurbon
victory g'alaba
video player videomagnitofon
videotape cassette videokasseta
view manzara
village qishloq
village elder oqsoqol
vinegar sirka; uksus
violence zo'ravonlik
virus virus
visa viza
visit *verb* ...-ga bor-; *as a guest* uyiga bor-
visitor mehmon
vodka aroq
voice tovush
voltage voltaj
vomit: I have been vomiting. Qusyapman.
vote *noun* ovoz; *verb* ovoz ber-
voting ovoz berish
vote-rigging ovoz berishning soxtalashtirilishi

wage war urush-
wait kut-
waiter ofitsant
wait for kut-
waitress ofitsantka
wake uyg'on-; **Please wake me up at ...** Soat ...da uyg'oting.
wake-up call uyg'otish uchun telefon

Wales Uels
walkie-talkie ratsiya
wall devor
wallet bumajnik
walnut yong'oq
want: What do you want? Sizga nima kerak?; **I want ...** Menga ... kerak.; **I don't want ...** Menga ... kerak emas.; **I want to leave.** Ketmoqchiman.
war urush; **civil war** fuqarolar urushi
war crime urush qoidalariga qarshi jinoyat
warm issiq; iliq
war tribunal urush tribunali
wash yuv-
wasp ari
watch *noun* soat; *verb* qara-
watchmaker's soatsozlik
water suv; **Is there drinking water?** Ichiladigan suv bormi?
water bottle suv shisha
waterfall shalola
watermelon tarvuz
wave to'lqin
way taraf; **this way** bu taraf; **that way** u taraf
we biz
weak kuchsiz
weapon qurol
wear kiy-
weasel latcha
weather havo
Wednesday chorshanba
week hafta; **last week** o'tgan hafta; **next week** keyingi hafta; **this week** bu hafta
weekend shanba-yakshanba
weep yig'la-
weight og'irlik
welcome! Marhamat!
well *adjective* sog'; *adverb* yaxshi; *noun* quduq; **oil well** neft qudug'i; **gas well** gaz qudug'i
well site quduq yeri
well-known mashhur

Welsh uelslik
west *noun* g'arb
west(ern) *adjective* g'arbiy
wet *adjective* suv; ho'l; *verb*
suvla-
what? nima?; **what kind?**
qanaqa?; **what's that?** Nima
u?
wheat bug'doy
wheel g'ildirak
wheelchair nogironlar aravachasi
when? qachon?
where? qayerda?; qayoqda?;
where from? qayerdan?;
Where are you from? Siz
qayerliksiz?
which? qaysi?
whisky viski
white oq
who? kim?
whole butun
why? nega?
wide keng
widow beva
widowed: I am widowed.
Bevaman.
widower beva
wife xotin
wild yovvoy
willow tol
win: Who won? Kim yutdi?
wind *noun* shamol
wind *verb* o'ra-
window deraza
windshield old oyna
windy: It's windy. Shamol
esyapti.
wine vino; sharob
wing qanot
winter qish
wire sim
wisdom hikmat
wish *verb* ista-; **I wish to ...**
...-shni istayman.
with bilan
withdraw chekin-; voz kech-

without -siz; **without water**
suvsiz
witness guvoh
wolf bo'ri
woman ayol; xotin kishi
womb qorin; bachadon
wonton chuchvara
wood *forest* daraxtzor; *substance*
yog'och
wool jun
word so'z
work *noun* ish; *verb* ishla-; **The
phone doesn't work.** Telefon
ishlamayapti.
worker ishchi
world dunyo
worm qurt; **earthworm** chuvalchang
worried: to be worried xavotir
ol-; qo'rq-
worse yomonroq; **I feel worse.**
Yomonroq his qilyapman.
worth foyda
wound *noun* yara; *verb* yarala-
wrapped o'ralgan
wrench *noun* gayka klyuchi
wrestling kurash
wrist bilak
write yoz-
writer yozuvchi
writing yozuv
writing paper (yozish uchun)
gog'oz
wrong noto'g'ri; **You're
wrong!** Gapingiz noto'g'ri.

X

X-ray rentgen

Y

yard bog'cha; hovli; *distance* yard
year yil; **last year** o'tgan yili;

yellow

this year bu yil; **next year**
keyingi yil; **the year after
next** ikki yildan keyin
yellow sariq
Yerevan Yerevan
yes ha
yesterday kecha; **the day
before yesterday** oldingi kun
yet hali
yield yo'l ber-
yogurt qatiq
you *singular* siz; *plural* sizlar
young yosh
young person yosh bola

your *singular* sizning; *plural*
sizlarning
yours *singular* sizniki; *plural*
sizlarniki
yourself o'zingiz
yourselves o'zinglar

Z

zero nul
zoo hayvonot bog'i; zoopark

UZBEK
Phrasebook

1. ETIQUETTE

Hello . . .

Assalomu alaykum! is the Uzbek way of saying "hello!",
to which the formal reply is **alaykum assalom!**, or simply
saying back **assalomu alaykum!** This greeting, which
means "peace on you!" is also used for the other greetings
of the day, corresponding to English "good morning," "good
afternoon," "good evening," and "good night."

how are you? | **yaxshimisiz?**
| *or* **ahvollar yaxshimi?**
| *or* **qalaysiz?**
fine, thank you! | **yaxshi, rahmat!**

see you tomorrow! | **ertagacha xayr!**
good bye! | **xayr!**
bon voyage! | **oq yo'l!**
welcome! | **marhamat!**
| **xush kelibsiz***

bon appetit! | **olinglar!****
thank you | **rahmat**
good luck! | **sizga omad!**
excuse me! | **kechirasiz!**

may I? | **mumkinmi?**
sorry! | **kechirasiz!**
| *or* **xafa bo'lmang!**
yes | **ha*****
no | **yo'q*****

* This is said only after you have sat down and exchanged
greetings with all present.
** The literal meaning is "help yourself!"
*** Also see the note on "yes" and "no" on page 158.

2. QUICK REFERENCE

I	**men**
you *singular*	**siz**
he/she/it	**u**
we	**biz**
you *plural*	**sizlar**
they	**ular**
this	**bu; shu**
that	**u; o'sha**
these	**bular**
those	**ular**
here	**bu yer(da)**
there	**u yer(da)**
where?	**qayer(da)?**
who?	**kim?**
what?	**nima?**
when?	**qachon?**
which?	**qaysi?**
how?	**qanday?; qanaqa?**
why?	**nimaga?; nega?**
how much?	**qancha?**
how many?	**necha(ta)?**
what's that?	**nima u?**
is there?/are there?	**. . . bormi?**
where is/are?	**. . . qayerda?**
	or **. . . qayoqda?**
What must I do?	**Men nima qilay?**
What do you want?	**Sizga nima kerak?**
very	**juda**
and	**bilan***
or	**yoki**
but	**lekin**

* Written Uzbek also uses the word **va**.

I like . . . *something*	**Menga . . . yoqadi.**
people and strong likes	**Men ...-ni yaxshi ko'raman.**
I don't like . . .	**Men . . .-ni yomon ko'raman.** *or* **Menga . . . yoqmaydi.**
I should like . . .	**. . .-gim kelyapti.**
I want . . . *something*	**Men . . . olmoqchiman.** *or* **Menga . . . kerak.**
I want to (leave).	**Men (ket)moqchiman.**
I don't want . . .	**Menga . . . kerak emas.**
I don't want to (leave).	**Men (ket)moqchi-masman.** *or* **(Ket)gim kelmayapti.**
I know.	**Bilaman.**
I don't know.	**Bilmadim.**
Do you understand?	**Tushunasizmi?**
I understand.	**Tushunaman.** *or* **Bilaman.**
I don't understand.	**Tushunmadim.** *or* **Bilmayman.**
I am sorry.	**Afsus!** *or* **Xafa bo'lmang!**
if someone falls ill	**Xudo shifosini bersin**.
if someone dies	**Bandachilik**.
It's important.	**Bu muhim narsa.**
It doesn't matter.	**Hech nima qilmaydi.**
You're welcome!	**Arzimaydi.**
I am grateful.	**Minnatdorman.**
No problem!	**Xo'p!**

QUICK REFERENCE

more or less	**taxminan**
here is/here are	**Mana . . .**
Is everything OK?	**Hamma narsa joyidami?**
danger!	**xavfli!**
How do you spell that?	**Qanaqa yoziladi?**

—Feelings

I am . . .

cold	**Men sovqotib ketdim.**
hot	**Men isib ketdim.**
right	**Meniki to'g'ri.**
sleepy	**Uyqim kelyapti.**
hungry	**Qornim och.**
thirsty	**Chanqab ketdim.**
angry	**Jahlim chiqyapti.**
happy	**Xursandman.**
sad	**Xafaman.**
tired	**Charchab ketdim.**
well	**Tuzukman.**

—Colors

black	**qora**
blue	**ko'k**
brown	**jigarrang**
green	**yashil; ko'k**
orange	**to'q sariq; qovoq rang**
pink	**pushti**
purple	**siyoh rang; binafsha rang**
red	**qizil**
white	**oq**
yellow	**sariq**

3. INTRODUCTIONS

What is your name?	**Otingiz nima?**
My name is . . .	**Otim . . .**
May I introduce you to . . .	**Sizni . . .-ga tanishtirib qo'ysam maylimi?**
This is my . . .	**Bu mening . . .**
friend	**o'rtog'im**
colleague/companion	**hamkasbim** *or* **hamkorlik qilyapmiz**
relative	**qarindoshim**

> **TITLES** — Uzbeks don't use titles such as "Mr." or "Mrs." Instead, people are referred to by **aka** (older males) or **opa** (older females), along with titles such as **domla** for a professor or teacher, or **doktor**, etc. **Aka** and **opa** are used following the person's first name, e.g. **Fred aka** and **Emma opa**.

▬Nationality

Where are you from?	**Qayerliksiz?**
I am from . . .	**Men . . . -danman.**
America	**Amerika**
Australia	**Avstraliya**
Britain	**Buyuk Britaniya**
Canada	**Kanada**
China	**Xitoy**
England	**Angliya**
Europe	**Yevropa**
Germany	**Germaniya**
India	**Hindiston**
Iran	**Eron**
Ireland	**Irlandiya**

INTRODUCTIONS

Japan	**Yaponiya**
New Zealand	**Yangizilandiya**
Northern Ireland	**Shimoliy Irlandiya**
Pakistan	**Pokiston**
Scotland	**Shotlandiya**
Wales	**Uels**
the USA	**Amerika**

I am . . .	**Men . . . -man.**
American	**amerikalik**
Australian	**avstraliyalik**
British	**britaniyalik**
Canadian	**kanadalik**
Chinese	**xitoy**
Dutch	**gollandiyalik**
English	**ingliz**
German	**nemis**
Indian	**hind**
Iranian	**eronlik**
Irish	**irlandiyalik**
Israeli	**isroillik**
Japanese	**yapon**
Pakistani	**pokistonlik**
Scottish	**shotlandiyalik**
Welsh	**uelslik**

Where were you born?	**Siz qayerda tug'ilgansiz?**
I was born in . . .	**. . .-da tug'ilganman.**

▬Central Asian nationalities

Afghan	**afg'on**
Armenian	**arman**
Azerbaijani	**ozarbayjon**
Chechen	**chechen**
Daghestani	**dog'istonlik**
Dungan (*Chinese Muslim*)	**dungon**
Georgian	**gruzin**

Jew	**jugut**
Kalmuk	**qalmoq**
Karakalpak	**qoraqalpoq**
Kazakh	**qozoq**
Kirghiz	**qirg'iz**
Korean	**kores**
Mongolian	**mo'g'ul**
Russian	**rus**
Tajik	**tojik**
Tatar	**tatar**
Tibetan	**tibetlik**
Turkmen	**turkman**
Uighur	**uyg'ur**
Ukrainian	**ukrain**

—Occupations

What do you do?	**Nima ish qilasiz?**
I am a/an . . .	**Men . . . man.**
	or **Men . . . bo'p ishlayman.**
academic	**akademik**
accountant	**buxgalter; hisobchi**
administrator	**administrator**
agronomist	**agronom**
aid worker	**beg'araz yordam xizmatchisi**
architect	**arxitektor; me'mor**
artist	**rassom**
business person	**biznesmen**
carpenter	**duradgor**
consultant	**maslahatchi**
dentist	**tish doktori**
diplomat	**elchi**
doctor	**doktor**
economist	**ekonomist; iqtisodchi**

engineer	**injener; muhandis**
farmer	**dehqon**
film-maker	**(kino)rejissyor**
journalist	**jurnalist; muxbir**
lawyer	**advokat; himoyachi**
mechanic	**mexanik**
negotiator	**muzokara olib boruvchi**
nurse	**hamshira; medsestra**
observer	**kuzatuvchi**
officer worker	**xodim (ofis xodimi)**
pilot	**pilot**
political scientist	**siyosatshunos**
scientist	**olim**
secretary	**kotib; sekretar**
soldier	**askar; soldat**
student *school*	**o'quvchi**
university	**student**
surgeon	**xirurg; jarroh**
teacher	**o'qituvchi; domla**
telecommunications specialist	**telealoqalar mutaxassisi**
tourist	**sayohatchi; turist**
writer	**yozuvchi**

—Age

How old are you?	**Yoshingiz nechada?** *or* **Necha yoshsiz?**
I am . . . years old.	**. . . yoshdaman.**

—Family

Are you married? *male*	**Uylanganmisiz?**
female	**Turmushga chiqqanmisiz?**
I am single. *male*	**Bo'ydoqman.** *or* **Uylanmaganman.**

INTRODUCTIONS

I am single.	*female*	**Turmushga chiqmaganman.**
I am married.	*male*	**Uylanganman.**
	female	**Turmushga chiqqanman.**
I am divorced.	*male*	**Xotinim bilan ajrashganman.**
	female	**Erim bilan ajrashganman.**
I am a widow/widower.		**Bevaman.**

Do you have a boyfriend?	**Yigitingiz bormi?**
Do you have a girlfriend?	**Yaxshi ko'radigan qizingiz bormi?**
What is his/her name?	**Uning oti nima?**

How many children do you have?	**Necha bolangiz bor?**
I don't have any children.	**Bolalarim yo'q.**
I have a daughter.	**Bitta qizim bor.**
I have a son.	**Bitta o'g'lim bor.**

How many brothers and sisters do you have?	**Oilada nechta bolasizlar?**
How many brothers do you have?	**Nechta aka-ukangiz bor?**
How many sisters do you have?	**Nechta opa-singlingiz bor?**

father	**dada**
mother	**oyi**
grandfather	**buva**
grandmother	**buvi**
older brother	**aka**
younger brother	**uka**
older sister	**opa**
younger sister	**singil**

children	**bolalar**
daughter	**qiz**
son	**o'g'il**
twins	**egizak**
husband	**er; xo'jayin**
wife	**xotin**
family	**oila**
man	**erkak kishi**
woman	**xotin kishi**
boy	**(o'g'il) bola**
girl	**qiz bola**
person	**shaxs**
people	**odamlar**

—Religion

The Uzbeks are Sunni Muslims. (For more, see the note on 'Religious Heritage' on page 150.)

What is your religion?	**Sizning diningiz nima?**
I am (a) . . .	**Men . . .**
Muslim	**musulmonman**
Buddhist	**buddistman**
Orthodox	**pravoslavman**
Christian	**xristianman**
Catholic	**katolikman**
Hindu	**hinduman**
Jewish	**yahudiyman**
I am not religious.	**Dindor emasman.**

LANGUAGE

4. LANGUAGE

Aside from other indigenous languages spoken in Central
Asia, almost everyone speaks Russian. Many will also know
a smattering at least of one or more European languages –
such as German and English. Because Uzbeks are
scattered over a wide area outside of the republics of
Central Asia, as well as due to the obvious influence of
Islam, you will find quite a few speakers of Tajik, Turkish,
and perhaps Arabic.

Do you speak English?	**Inglizcha bilasizmi?**
Do you speak Russian?	**Ruscha bilasizmi?**
Do you speak German?	**Nemischa bilasizmi?**
Do you speak French?	**Frantsuzcha bilasizmi?**
Do you speak Farsi?	**Forscha bilasizmi?**
Do you speak Chinese?	**Xitoycha bilasizmi?**
Does anyone speak English?	**Inglizcha biladigan bormi?**
I speak a little . . .	**Ozgina . . . bilaman.**
I don't speak . . .	**. . . bilmayman.**
I understand.	**Tushunaman.**
I don't understand.	**Tushunmayman.**
Please point to the word in the book.	**Kitobda yozilganini ko'rsating.**
Please wait while I look up the word.	**Kerakli so'zni qidiryotganimda turib turing.**
Please could you speak more slowly.	**Sal sekinroq gapiring.**
Could you repeat that?	**Qaytarvoring. Nima dedingiz?**
How do you say . . . in Uzbek?	**O'zbekchada . . . qanday aytiladi?**

What does . . . mean?	**. . . degani nima degani?**
How do you pronounce this word?	**Bu so'z qanaqa aytiladi?**
I speak . . .	**Men . . . bilaman.**
Arabic	**arabcha**
Armenian	**armancha**
Azeri	**ozarbayjoncha**
Chechen	**chechen tilini**
Chinese	**xitoycha**
Danish	**daniyaliklar tilini**
Dutch	**gollanda tilini**
English	**inglizcha**
Farsi	**forscha**
French	**frantsuzcha**
Georgian	**gruzincha**
German	**nemischa**
Greek	**grek tilini**
Italian	**italyancha**
Japanese	**yaponcha**
Kazakh	**qozoqcha**
Kirghiz	**qirg'izcha**
Mongolian	**mo'g'il tilini**
Russian	**ruscha**
Spanish	**ispancha**
Tajik	**tojikcha**
Tibetan	**tibet tilini**
Turkish	**turkcha**
Turkmen	**turkmancha**
Ukrainian	**ukraincha**

5. BUREAUCRACY

> Note that many forms you encounter may be written in Russian instead.

name	**ism**
surname	**familiya**
middle name	**otaning ismi**
address	**adres; manzil**
date of birth	**tug'ilgan kun**
place of birth	**tug'ilgan joy**
nationality	**fuqarolik**
age	**yosh**
sex	**jins**
male	**er**
female	**xotin**
religion	**din**
reason for travel	**sayohat qilishdan maqsad**
business	**tijorat**
tourism	**turizm; sayohat**
work	**ish**
personal	**shaxsiy**
profession	**kasb**
marital status	**oilaviy holati**
single *male*	**uylanmagan; bo'ydoq**
female	**turmushga chiqmagan**
married *male*	**uylangan**
female	**turmushga chiqqan**
divorced	**er/xotindan ajrashgan**
date	**sana; chislo**
date of arrival	**kelish muddati**
date of departure	**ketish muddati**
passport	**pasport**

passport number	**pasport nomeri**
visa	**viza**
currency	**pul**

Is this the correct form?	**Kerakli hujjat shumi?**
What does this mean?	**Bu nima degani?**
Where is . . .'s office?	**. . .-ning ofisi qayerda?**
Which floor is it on?	**Nechanchi qavatda?**
Does the elevator work?	**Lift ishlayaptimi?**

Is Mr/Ms . . . in?	**. . . bormi?**
Please tell him/her that I am here.	**Ularga men keldi deb ayting.**
I can't wait, I have an appointment.	**Men kutolmayman, boshqa joyda uchrashuvim bor.**
Tell him/her that I was here.	**Men kelib ketdi deb aytib qo'ying.**

▬Ministries

Ministry of Agriculture	**Qishloq Xo'jaligi Vazirligi**
Ministry of Defense	**Mudofaa Vazirligi**
Ministry of Education	**Xalq Ta'limi Vazirligi**
Ministry of Foreign Affairs	**Tashqi Ishlar Vazirligi**
Ministry of Health	**Sog'liqni Saqlash Vazirligi**
Ministry of Internal Affairs	**Ichki Ishlar Vazirligi**
Ministry of Justice	**Adliya Vazirligi**

6. TRAVEL

PUBLIC TRANSPORT — Buses or trolley buses can often be too packed for comfort, but Tashkent's metro is quite good. There are numerous minibuses called **marshrutka**, which stop at pre-determined pickup points. You pay the driver or his assistant as you get out. Buses are reliable and leave from specially designated areas. Intercity buses usually wait to collect the most possible number of passengers. Travel by rail is slow and subject to long delays mid-journey. Note that all public announcements, particularly for trains and planes, are made both in Uzbek and Russian (and Tajik in Samarqand and Bukhara). Bicycles and motorbikes are not difficult to find but are not used much in city areas.

What time does . . . leave/arrive?	**. . . qachon keladi/yuradi?**
the airplane	**samolyo't**
the boat	**paroxod**
the bus	**avtobus**
the train	**poezd**
the trolley bus	**trolleybus**
The plane is delayed/canceled.	**Samolyo't kechikadi./ Reys bekor qilindi.**
The train is delayed/canceled.	**Poezd kechikadi./ Bekor qilindi.**
How long will it be delayed?	**Necha soat kech keladi?**
There is a delay of . . . minutes/hours.	**. . . minut/soat kech keladi.**
Excuse me, where is the ticket office?	**Kassa qayoqda?**
Where can I buy a ticket?	**Qayerdan bilet olsam bo'ladi?**
I want to go to . . .	**. . .-ga bormoqchiman.**
I want a ticket to . . .	**. . .-ga bilet olmoqchiman.**

I would like . . .	. . .-ni olmoqchiman.
a one-way ticket	borish bileti
a return ticket	borish-kelish bileti
first class	birinchi klas
second class	ikkinchi klas
business class	biznes klas

Do I pay in dollars or in som?	Dollar bilan to'laymanmi, so'm bilanmi?
You must pay in dollars.	Dollar bilan to'lash kerak.
You must pay in som.	So'm bilan to'lash kerak.
You can pay in either.	Farqi yo'q.
Can I reserve a place?	Bir joyni bron qilsam bo'ladimi?
How long does the trip take?	Necha soatda boramiz?
Is it a direct route?	To'xtamasdan boradimi?

—Air

In Uzbekistan all flights are (technically) non-smoking.

Is there a flight to . . . ?	. . .-ga samolyo't bormi?
When is the next flight to . . . ?	. . .-ga keyingi samolyo't qachon uchadi?
How long is the flight?	Necha soatda yetib boradi?

TRAVEL

What is the flight number?	**Nechanchi reys?**
You must check in at . . .	**. . .-da ro'yxatdan o'tishingiz kerak.**
Is the flight delayed?	**Samolyo't kechikdimi?**
How many hours is the flight delayed?	**Necha soat kechikadi?**
Is this the flight for . . . ?	**Bu . . .-ga uchadigan samolyo'tmi?**
Is that the flight from . . . ?	**Bu . . . dan kelgan samolyo'tmi?**
When is the Moscow flight arriving?	**Moskvadan samolyo't qachon keladi?**
Is it on time?	**Vaqtida keladimi?**
Is it late?	**Kech keladimi?**
Do I have to change planes?	**Boshqa samolyo'tga o'tish kerakmi?**
Has the plane left Moscow yet?	**Moskvaga uchadigan samolyo't ketdimi?**
What time does the plane take off?	**Samolyo't qachon uchadi?**
What time do we arrive in Moscow?	**Moskvaga qachon yetib boramiz?**
excess baggage	**ortiqcha bagaj**
international flight	**xalqaro reys**
national flight	**ichki reys**

—Bus

bus stop	**bekat; ostanovka**
Where is the bus stop/ station?	**Ostanovka/ avtostantsiya qayoqda?**
Take me to the bus station.	**Meni avtostantsiyaga oborib qo'ying.**
Which bus goes to . . . ?	**Qaysi avtobus . . .-ga boradi?**

Does this bus go to . . . ?	**Bu avtobus . . .-ga boradimi?**
How often do buses pass by?	**Avtobuslar tez-tez kelib turadimi?**
What time is the . . . bus?	**. . .-ga boradigan avtobus qachon yuradi?**
next	**keyingi**
first	**birinchi**
last	**oxirgi**
Will you let me know when we get to . . . ?	**Biz . . .-ga kelganimizda menga aytasizmi?**
Stop, I want to get off!	**To'xtang!** *or* **Tushadiganlar bor!**
Where can I get a bus to . . . ?	**. . .-ga boradigan avtobusga qayerda chiqsam bo'ladi?**
When is the first bus to . . . ?	**. . .-ga ketadigan birinchi avtobus qachon bo'ladi?**
When is the last bus to . . . ?	**. . .-ga boradigan eng oxirgi avtobus qachon bo'ladi?**
When is the next bus to . . . ?	**. . .-ga boradigan keyingi avtobus qachon bo'ladi?**
Do I have to change buses?	**Boshqa avtobusga o'tish kerakmi?**
I want to get off at . . .	**. . . da tushmoqchiman.**
Please let me off at the next stop.	**Keyingi ostanovkada tushaman.**
Please let me off here.	**Shu yerda tushaman.**
How long is the journey?	**Ko'p yurish kerakmi?** *or* **Uzoqmi?**

What is the fare?	**Qancha to'lash kerak?**
I need my luggage, please.	**Yuklarimni olmoqchiman.**
That's my bag.	**Ana u sumka meniki.**

—Rail

Passengers must . . .	**Yo'lovchilar. . .**
change trains.	**boshqa poezdga o'tishlari kerak.**
change platforms.	**. . . boshqa perronga o'tishlari kerak.**
Is this the right platform for . . . ?	**Bu . . .-ga boradigan perronmi?**
The train leaves from platform . . .	**Poezdga . . . perrondan chiqiladi.**
Take me to the railway station.	**Vokzalga oborib qo'ying.**
Which platform should I go to?	**Qaysi perronga borishim kerak?**
platform one/two	**birinchi/ikkinchi perron**
You must change trains at . . .	**. . . da boshqa poezdga o'tish kerak.**
Where can I buy tickets?	**Biletni qayerdan olsam bo'ladi?**
Is there a timetable?	**Jadval bormi?**
Will the train leave on time?	**Poezd vaqtida yuradimi?**

| There will be a delay of . . . minutes. | . . . minut kechikadi. |
| There will be a delay of . . . hours. | . . . soat kechikadi. |

—Taxi

Some taxis are marked while others are not. You can also wave down and negotiate a fare with any private car willing to go your way, although this is not always as safe. To avoid unpleasant surprises, agree to fares in advance. It is useful to be able to tell the driver your destination in Uzbek or Russian (or have it written down on a piece of paper). Be warned, however, that some drivers will have as little idea as you as to the precise whereabouts of your destination. A reliable option is to call up one of the growing number of radio taxi companies.

Taxi!	Taksi!
Where can I get a taxi?	Qayerda taksiga chiqsam bo'ladi?
Please could you get me a taxi.	Menga taksi chaqirib bering.
Can you take me to . . . ?	. . .-ga borasizmi?
Please take me to . . .	Meni . . .-ga oboring.
How much will it cost to . . . ?	. . .-ga qancha bo'ladi?
To this address, please.	Shu adresga oborib qo'ying.
Turn left.	Chapga buriling.
Turn right.	O'ngga buriling.
Go straight ahead.	To'g'riga yuravering.
Stop!	To'xtang!
Don't stop!	To'xtamang!
I'm in a hurry.	Shoshyapman.
Please drive more slowly!	Sekinroq haydang, iltimos!

Here is fine, thank you.	**Shu yer bo'ladi, rahmat.**
The next corner, please.	**Keyingi ko'chagacha yuring.**
The next street to the left.	**Keyingi chap tomondagi ko'cha.**
The next street to the right.	**Keyingi o'ng tomondagi ko'cha.**
Stop here!	**Shu yerda to'xtang.**
Stop the car, I want to get out.	**To'xtatavoring, men tushaman.**
Please wait here.	**Shu yerda turib turing.**
Take me to the airport.	**Meni aeroportga oborib qo'ying.**

—General phrases

I want to get off at . . .	**. . . da tushmoqchiman.**
Excuse me!	**Kechirasiz!**
Excuse me, may I get by?	**Kechirasiz, men o'tvolay!**
These are my bags.	**Mana mening sumkalarim.**
Please put them there.	**Shu yerga qo'ying.**
Is this seat free?	**Bu joy bo'shmi?**
I think that's my seat.	**Bu mening joyim bo'lsa kerak.**

—Extra words

airport	**aeroport**
airport tax	**aeroport solig'i**
ambulance	**tez yordam mashinasi**
arrivals	**kelish jadvali**

baggage counter	**bagaj; yuk bo'limi; yuk kamerasi**
bicycle	**velosiped**
boarding pass	**o'tirish taloni**
boat	**paroxod**
bus stop	**ostanovka; bekat**
car	**mashina**
check-in	**registratsiya**
check-in counter	**ro'yxatdan o'tish joyi; registratsiya bo'limi**
closed	**yopiq**
customs	**bojxona**
delay	**kechikish**
departures	**ketish jadvali**
dining car	**vagon-restoran**
emergency exit	**avariya holatida chiqish**
entrance	**kirish**
exit	**chiqish**
express	**ekspres**
ferry	**parom**
4-wheel drive *vehicle*	**jip**
information	**ma'lumot**
ladies/gents	**ayollar/erkaklar**
local	**mahalliy**
helicopter	**vertolyo't**
horse and cart	**ot aravasi**
motorbike	**mototsikl**
no entry	**kirish mumkin emas**
no smoking	**chekish mumkin emas**
open	**ochiq**
platform number	**perron raqami**
radio taxi	**radioli taksi**
railway	**temir yo'l**
reserved	**bronlangan**
road	**yo'l**

TRAVEL

sign	**lavha; viveska**
sleeping car	**yotoq vagon;**
	spalniy vagon
station	**vokzal**
bus station	**avtovokzal**
subway	**metro**
telephone	**telefon**
ticket office	**kassa**
timetable	**jadval**
toilet(s)	**hojatxona; tualet**
town center	**shahar markazi**
train station	**vokzal**
trolley bus	**trolleybus**

ACCOMMODATION

7. ACCOMMODATION

Aside from the main hotels, which are mostly in Tashkent,
Samarqand, Bukhara, and Khiva and provide service to
European/US standards, you will find that room service is
not always available, and breakfast or other meals will have
to be negotiated and paid for separately. An excellent option
in more rural areas is to have your accommodation
arranged at a private house, where traditional hospitality
will guarantee that you are well looked after and, as always
in Uzbekistan, well fed. Note that **mehmonxona** means
'guesthouse' and 'hostel' as well as 'hotel'.

I am looking for a hotel. **Men mehmonxona qidiryapman.**

Is there anywhere I can
stay for the night? **Bir kechalik joy bormi?**

Where is . . . **. . . qayerda?**
or **. . . bormi?**

a cheap hotel **arzon mehmonxona**
a good hotel **yaxshi mehmonxona**

a nearby hotel **yaqinroq mehmonxona**

a clean hotel **toza mehmoxona**

What is the address? **Adresi qanaqa?**
Could you write the
address please? **Adresni yozib berolasizmi?**

▬At the hotel
Do you have any rooms
free? **Bo'sh xonalaringiz bormi?**
I would like . . . **Men . . . olmoqchiman.**
a single room **bir kishilik xona**

a double room	**ikki kishilik xona**
We'd like a room.	**Bizga bitta xona kerak.**
We'd like two rooms.	**Bizga ikkita xona kerak.**
I want a room with . . .	**Menga . . . xona kerak.**
a bathroom	**hojatxonali**
a shower	**dushli**
a television	**televizorli**
a window	**derazali**
a double bed	**ikki kishilik karavotli**
a balcony	**balkonli**
a view	**yaxshi manzarali**
I want a room that's quiet.	**Tinch xona kerak.**
How long will you be staying?	**Necha kun turasiz?**
How many nights?	**Necha kecha turasiz?**
I'm going to stay for . . .	**Men . . . turaman.**
one day	**bir kecha**
two days	**ikki kecha**
one week	**bir hafta**
Do you have any I.D.?	**Hujjatingiz bormi?** *or* **Dokumentingiz bormi?**
Sorry, we're full.	**Kechirasiz, bizda joy yo'q.**
I have a reservation.	**Joyni bronlaganman.**
My name is . . .	**Ismim . . .**
May I speak to the manager please?	**Direktor bilan gaplashsam bo'ladimi?**
I have to meet someone here.	**Bu yerda bittasi bilan uchrashishim kerak.**
How much is it per night?	**Bir kishi uchun qancha turadi?**

How much is it per week?	**Bir hafta qancha turadi?**
How much is it per person?	**Bir kecha qancha turadi?**
It's . . . per day/per person.	**Bir kishi uchun/bir kun . . . turadi.**
Can I see it?	**Ko'rsam maylimi?**
Are there any others?	**Boshqasi yo'qmi?**
Is there . . . ?	**. . . bormi?**
air conditioning	**konditsionir**
a telephone	**telefon**
hot water	**issiq suv**
laundry service	**kir yuvib berish xizmati**
room service	**xonani tozalash xizmati**
No, I don't like it.	**Menga yoqmadi.**
It's too . . .	**Juda . . .**
cold	**sovuq**
hot	**issiq**
big	**katta**
dark	**qorong'i**
small	**kichkina**
noisy	**shovqinli**
dirty	**iflos**
It's fine, I'll take it.	**Yaxshi, bo'ladi.**
Where is the bathroom?	**Tualet qayerda?**
Is there hot water all day?	**Kun bo'yi issiq suv bormi?**
Do you have a safe?	**Seyf bormi?**
Is there anywhere to wash clothes?	**Kir yuvsa bo'ladigan joy bormi?**
Can I use the telephone?	**Telefon qilsam bo'ladimi?**

ACCOMMODATION

▬Needs

I need . . .	**Menga . . . kerak.**
candles	**sham**
toilet paper	**tualet qog'ozi**
soap	**sovun**
clean sheets	**toza choyshab**
an extra blanket	**yana bitta adyol**
drinking water	**toza suv**
a light bulb	**lampochka**
Please change the sheets.	**Toza choyshabga almashtirb bering.**
I can't open the window.	**Derazani ocholmayapman.**
I can't close the window.	**Derazani yopolmayapman.**
I have lost my key.	**Kalitimni yo'qotib qo'ydim.**
Can I have the key to my room?	**Kalitni olsam maylimi?**
The toilet won't flush.	**Tualet ishlamayapti.**
The water has been cut off.	**Suv to'xtab qoldi.**
The electricity has been cut off.	**Svet o'chdi.**
The gas has been cut off.	**Gaz tugadi.**
The heating has been cut off.	**Otopleniye o'chirildi.**
The heater doesn't work.	**Batareyka ishlamayapti.**
The air conditioning doesn't work.	**Konditsioner ishlamayapti.**
The phone doesn't work.	**Telefon ishlamayapti.**
I can't flush the toilet.	**Tualetda suv tushmayapti.**

ACCOMMODATION

The toilet is blocked.	**Tualetda suv tiqilib qoldi.**
I can't switch off the tap.	**Kranni bekitolmayapman.**
I need a plug for the bath.	**Vannaga probka kerak.**
Where is the electric socket?	**Rozetka qayerda?**
wake-up call	**uyg'otish uchun telefon**
Could you please wake me up at . . . o'clock.	**Meni soat . . .-da uyg'oting.**
I am leaving now.	**Ketmoqchiman.**
We are leaving now.	**Ketmoqchimiz.**
May I pay the bill now?	**Hozir to'lasam maylimi?**

▬Extra words

bathroom	**tualet; hojatxona**
bed	**karavot**
blanket	**adyol**
candle	**sham**
chair	**stul**
cold water	**sovuq suv**
cupboard	**shkaf**
doorlock	**qulf**
electricity	**svet**
excluded	**. . .-ga kirmaydi.**
fridge	**xolodil'nik**
hot water	**issiq suv**
included	**. . . ichida; . . .-ga kiradi**
key	**kalit**
laundry service	**kir yuvish (xizmati)**
mattress	**matras**

ACCOMMODATION

meals/food	**ovqat**
mirror	**oyna**
name	**ism; ot**
noisy	**shovqinli**
padlock	**qulf**
pillow	**yostiq**
plug (bath)	**probka; tiqin**
plug (electric)	**plugshtepsel vilkasi**
quiet	**tinch**
room	**xona**
room number	**xona nomeri**
sheet	**choyshab**
shower	**dush**
suitcase	**chamadon**
surname	**familiya**
table	**stol**
towel	**sochiq**
water	**suv**
window	**deraza**

8. FOOD & DRINK

Food plays an important part of Uzbek life, and important events in all aspects of life and the seasons are marked with foods of different kinds. Food is a very important aspect of Uzbek hospitality; it is both the host's duty to make sure his guests are eating and the guest's duty to partake of what is offered. **Pilau** is king in Uzbek cuisine, and new guests are traditionally fed this rice dish above all others.

breakfast	**(ertalabki) choy**
lunch	**obed** *or* **tushlik**
dinner, supper	**kechki ovqat**
dessert	**shirinlik** *or* **desert**

MEALS — Uzbeks do not use separate names for meals as in English. The terms given above are rather literal terms. Breakfast is referred to as 'tea', as in **choyga kelinglar** — though this could refer to any other tea time. Lunch and dinner are usually just called **ovqat** 'food'. The verb **ovqatlanish** refers to eating lunch, dinner, or any other large meal.

I'm hungry.	**Qornim ochdi.**
I'm thirsty.	**Chanqab ketdim.**
Have you eaten yet?	**Ovqatlandingizmi?**
Do you know a good restaurant?	**Yaxshi restoran qayerda, bilasizmi?**
Do you have a table, please?	**Bo'sh stol bormi?**
I would like a table for . . . people, please.	**. . . kishi uchun stol bormi?**
Can I see the menu please?	**Menyuni ko'rsam maylimi?**
I'm still looking at the menu.	**Haliyam menyuni o'qiyapman.**
I would like to order now.	**. . . olaman.**

FOOD & DRINK

What's this?	**Bu nima?**
Is it spicy?	**Achchiqmi?**
Does it have meat in it?	**Ichida go'sht bormi?**
Does it have alcohol in it?	**Ichida spirt bormi?**
Do you have . . . ?	**. . . bormi?**
We don't have . . .	**. . . yo'q.**
What would you recommend?	**Nimalaringiz yaxshi?**
Do you want . . . ?	**. . . yeysizmi?**
	or **. . . olasizmi?**
Can I order some more . . . ?	**Yana . . . olsam bo'ladimi?**
That's all, thank you.	**Bo'ldi, rahmat.**
I haven't finished yet.	**Hali yeb bo'lmadim.**
I have finished eating.	**Bo'ldim.**
I am full!	**To'yib ketdim!**
Where are the toilets?	**Tualet qayoqda?**
I am a vegetarian.*	**Vegeterianman.**
I don't eat meat.*	**Go'sht yemayman.**
I don't eat pork.	**Cho'chqa go'shti yemayman.**
I don't eat chicken or fish.*	**Tovuq bilan baliq yemayman.**
I don't drink alcohol.	**Spirtli ichimliklarni ichmayman.** *or* **Aroq ichmayman.**
I don't smoke.	**Chekmayman.**

CULTURAL NOTE — While in the West it is perfectly OK to state dietary preferences, in Uzbek society this is interpreted as an insult to the host: you are in effect telling them that the food isn't good enough for you. In traditional Uzbek society (and many other Asian societies) people will be baffled that someone would voluntarily choose not to eat meat.

FOOD & DRINK

I would like . . .	. . . opkeling.
an ashtray	kuldon
the bill	kvitansiya
a glass of water	bir stakan suv
a bottle of water	bir shisha suv
a bottle of wine	bir shisha sharob/vino
a bottle of beer	bitta pivo
another bottle	yana bir shisha
a bottle-opener	shisha ochadigan
a corkscrew	probka ochadigan
dessert	desert; shirinlik
a drink *non-alcoholic*	ichimlik
a fork	vilka
another chair	yana bir stul
another plate	yana bir tarelka
another glass	yana bir stakan
another cup	yana bir piyola; chashka
a napkin	salfetka
a glass	stakan
a knife	pichoq
a plate	tarelka
a samovar	samovar
a spoon	qoshiq
a table	stol
a teaspoon	choy qoshig'i
a toothpick	tish tozalaydigan
fresh	yangi; svezhiy
spicy (hot)	achchiq
stale	suvi qochgan
sour	nordon
sweet	shirin
bitter	achchiq
hot	issiq

FOOD & DRINK

cold	**sovuq**
salty	**sho'r**
tasteless	**bemaza**
tasty	**shirin; mazali**
bad/spoiled	**buzilgan**
too much	**ko'p**
too little	**kam**
not enough	**yetarli emas**

—Food

bread	*flat*	**non**
	loaf	**buxonka non**
candy		**konfet**
caviar		**ikra**
cheese		**sir; pishloq**
chewing gum		**saqich; zvochka**
egg		**tuxum**
flour		**un**
french fries		**salomka**
hamburger		**gamburger**
honey		**asal**
ice cream		**morozhniy; muz qaymoq**
ketchup		**ketchup**
mustard		**gorchitsa**
nut		**mag'iz**
	almond	**bodom**
	pistachio	**pista**
	salty apricot pits	**sho'rdonak**
	walnut	**yong'oq**
oil		**yog'**
pasta		**makaron**
black pepper		**qora murch**
hot pepper		**garmdori**
pizza		**pitsa**
salad		**salat**

FOOD & DRINK

salt	**tuz**
sandwich	**buterbrod**
soup	**sho'rva**
sugar	**shakar**
vinegar	**sirka; uksus**
yogurt	**qatiq**

> **RICE** — **Guruch** is uncooked rice. All cooked rice in Uzbek cuisine becomes pilau (**palov**) or some other term depending on the dish. It's not eaten as plain white rice.

▬Vegetables

beetroot	**qizilcha**
cucumber	**bodring**
potato	**kartoshka**
pepper	**qalampir**
tomato	**pomidor**
vegetables	**sabzavot**

▬Fruit

apple	**olma**
grape	**uzum**
lemon	**limon**
melon	**qovun**
orange	**apel'sin**
peach	**shaftoli**
persimmon	**xurmo**
plum	**olxo'ri**
sour plum	**ko'k sulton**
strawberry	**qulupnay**
watermelon	**tarvuz**

▬Meat

beef	**mol go'shti**
chicken	**tovuq**

FOOD & DRINK

fish		baliq
kebab	*chunks of meat*	shashlik
	ground meat	kabob
lamb		qo'y go'shti
pork		cho'chqa go'shti
sausage/hot dog		sosiska

—Drinks

Remember to ask for modern soft drinks by brand name.

alcohol(ic drinks)	spirt(li ichimliklar)
beer	pivo
bottle	shisha
brandy	konyak
can	banka
champagne	shampanskiy
coffee	kofe; qahva
coffee with milk	sutli kofe
cognac	konyak
fruit juice	meva sharbati; meva suvi
ice	muz
milk	sut
mineral water	Toshkent suvi; mineral suv
tea	choy
tea with lemon	limonli choy
tea with milk	sutli choy
no sugar, please	shakarsiz
vodka	aroq
water	suv
whisky	viski
wine	sharob; vino
red	qizil sharob
sparkling	gazli sharob
white	oq sharob

More on food & drink . . .

Food in Uzbekistan is a great discovery for the visitor. Each part of Uzbekistan has its unique cuisine with its own special flavor. There is a wide variety of rice and noodle-based dishes, and several varieties of soups. Some dishes are obviously Iranian in origin, some Chinese. Some common specialities include:

palov; osh — pilau made from lamb or beef cooked with carrots, onions, and spices, especially garlic and cumin

chuchvara — wonton dumplings served with either tomato or yogurt

do'lma – grape leaves, cabbage, or peppers stuffed with ground lamb and spices

somsa — small oven-baked meat pies filled with meat, onions and fat

manti — steamed meat pies

dimlama — meat, potatoes and vegetables steamed in their own juices

lag'mon — long noodles served in soup

Accompanying the above will be seasonal greens and other finger food. Finish off your meal with fruit — Uzbekistan is famous for its melons and grapes, all washed down with the ubiquitous tea or mineral water bottled from one of the country's many natural sources.

ALCOHOL — Alcohol is drunk commonly, but one may encounter disapproval in some cases for religious reasons, which should be respected. Once started, though, you will be asked to drink more and more!

FEASTING — Uzbeks have developed a finely tuned tradition of feasting through the **ziyofat**, or banquet. Course after course is brought to a low table around which the diners sit. The only essential phrases to know here: **Xush kelibsizlar!** 'Welcome!'

ETIQUETTE — Each meal (or any other gathering) ends with a small prayer or **fotiha** during which everyone holds out their hands, then strokes their face before getting up to leave.

9. DIRECTIONS

Where is . . . ?	. . . qayerda/qayoqda?
the academy	akademiya
the airport	aeroport
the art gallery	san'at galereyasi
a bank	bank
the church	cherkov
the city center	shahar markazi
the consulate	konsulxona
the . . . embassy	. . . elchixonasi
the hotel	mehmonxona
the information office	ma'lumotlar byurosi
the main square	skver; maydon
the market	bozor
the Ministry of . . .	. . . vazirligi
the mosque	machit
the museum	muzey
parliament	parlament
Uzbek parliament	Oliy Majlis
the police station	militsiya uchastkasi
the post office	pochta
the railway station	vokzal
the synagogue	senago'g
the telephone center	telefon markazi; telegraf
a toilet	tualet; hojatxona
the university	universitet

Where . . . ?

There are three basic ways of asking 'where?' in Uzbek. There is some overlap in usage, but the basic differences are as follows:

—**Qayerda?** is used when asking the location of something, as on a map. **"Nyu Yo'rk qayerda?"** **"Amerikada."** ("Where is New York?" "In America.")

—**Qayoqda?** (or **qaysi tomonda/tarafda?**) is used when asking which direction you should head to find something, as when searching for a store or address when you're in the vicinity: **"Pochta qayoqda?"** "Where/which way is the post office?"
—**Qani?** is used to ask the whereabouts of a person or thing that should be present or at hand, as in asking where your keys are: **"Kalitlarim qani?"**

What . . . is this?	**Bu qaysi . . . ?**
bridge	**ko'prik**
building	**bino**
city	**shahar**
district	**rayon**
river	**daryo**
road	**yo'l**
street	**ko'cha**
town	**posyolka**
village	**qishloq**

What is this building?	**Bu bino nima?**
What is that building?	**Ana u bino nima?**
What time does it open?	**Qachon ochiladi?**
What time does it close?	**Qachon yopiladi?**
Can I park here?	**Mashinamni shu yerda qoldirsam bo'ladimi?**
Are we on the right road for . . . ?	**Bu yo'l . . .-ga boradimi?**
How many kilometers is it to . . . ?	**. . .-gacha necha kilometr?**
It is . . . kilometers away.	**. . . kilometr bor.**
How far is the next village?	**Bundan keyingi qishloq uzoqmi?**
Where can I find this address?	**Shu joy qayerda?**
Can you show me on the map?	**Xaritadan/kartadan ko'rsatvoring.**
How do I get to . . . ?	**. . .-ga qanaqa borsam bo'ladi?**

DIRECTIONS

I want to go to . . .	. . .-ga bormoqchiman.
Can I walk there?	Yayov borsam bo'ladimi?
Is it far?	Uzoqmi?
Is it near?	Yaqinmi?
Is it far from/near here?	Shu yerdan uzoqmi?
It is not far.	Uzoq emas.
Go straight ahead.	To'griga yuring.
It's two blocks down.	Ikki ostanovkadan* keyin.
Turn left.	Chapga buriling (qayriling).
Turn right.	O'ngga buriling.
at the next corner	bundan keyingi burchakda
at the traffic lights	svetoforda
behind	. . . orqasida
far	uzoq
in front of	. . . oldida
left	chap (tomon)
near	yaqin
opposite	. . . to'g'risida
right	o'ng (tomon)
straight on	to'g'ri(ga)
bridge	ko'prik
corner	burchak
crossroads	perekroystka
one-way street	bir tomonlama yo'l
north	shimol
south	janub
east	sharq
west	g'arb

* Distance along streets is measured in bus stops (**ostanovka**), not city blocks.

10. SHOPPING

Where can I find a . . . ?	**. . . qayerda bo'ladi?**
Where can I buy . . . ?	**. . . qayerda olsam bo'ladi?**
Where's the market?	**Bozor qayoqda?**
Where's the nearest . . . ?	**Eng yaqin . . . qayoqda?**
Please can you help me.	**Menga qarashavoring.**
Can I help you?	**Sizga nima kerak?**
I'm just looking.	**Shundoq qarayapman.**
I'd like to buy . . .	**. . . olmoqchiman.**
Could you show me some . . . ?	**Menga . . . ko'rsatolasizmi?**
Can I look at it?	**. . . ko'rsam maylimi?**
Do you have any . . . ?	**. . . bormi?**
This.	**Mana bu.**
That.	**Mana shu.**
I like it.	**Menga yoqdi.**
I don't like it.	**Menga yoqmadi.**
Do you have anything cheaper?	**Arzonrog'i bormi?**
cheaper/better	**arzonroq/yaxshiroq**
larger/smaller	**kattaroq/kichkinaroq**
Do you have anything else?	**Yana boshqa narsalar bormi?**
Do you have any others?	**Boshqasi bormi?**
Sorry, this is the only one.	**Yo'q, bundan boshqasi yo'q.**

SHOPPING

I'll take it.	**Xo'p, oldim.**
How much/many do you want?	**Qancha/nechta olasiz?**
How much is it?	**Necha pul?**
Can you write down the price?	**Narxini yozib berolasizmi?**
Could you lower the price?	**Arzonroq qilolmaysizmi?**
I don't have much money.	**Ko'p pulim yo'q.**
Do you take credit cards?	**Kredit kartochkalarni olasizmi?**
Would you like it wrapped?	**O'rab beraymi?**
Will that be all?	**Yana boshqa narsa olasizmi?** *or* **Bo'ldimi?**
Thank you, good-bye.	**Rahmat.**
I want to return this.	**Mana buni qaytarib bermoqchiman.**

—Outlets

baker's	**non do'koni**
bank	**bank**
barber's	**sartaroshxona**
I'd like a haircut please.	**Sochimni kaltalatmoqchiman.**
bookshop	**kitob do'koni**
butcher's	**go'sht do'koni**
car spares outlet	**zapchast/ehtiyot qismlar do'koni**
pharmacy	**apteka; dorixona**
clothes shop	**kiyim-kechak do'koni**
dairy goods store	**sutli mahsulotlar do'koni**
dentist	**tish doktori**
department store	**magazin**
dressmaker	**tikuvchi**

electrical goods store	**elektron buyumlar do'koni**
florist	**gul do'koni**
greengrocer	**sabzavot do'koni**
hairdresser	**ayollar sartaroshxonasi**
haircut/hairdo	**prichyoska**
hardware store	**xo'jalik mollari do'koni**
hospital	**bolnitsa; kasalxona**
kiosk	**kiosk**
laundry room	**kir yuvish xonasi**
market	**bozor**
newsstand	**gazeta sotadigan kiosk**
shoeshop	**poyafzal do'koni**
shop	**do'kon**
souvenir shop	**yodgorliklar do'koni**
stationer's	**kantselyariya do'koni**
supermarket	**supermarket**
travel agent	**sayohat agentligi**
vegetable shop	**sabzavot do'koni**
watchmaker's	**soatsozlik**

—Gifts

ARTS AND CRAFTS — Uzbekistan boasts numerous artists of varying quality and there are a number of antique shops notably in Tashkent's **Eski Shahar** (Old City) Remember that there are restrictions on what you can take out of the country. Buying art is little problem as every Uzbek seems to have a friend who is an artist or craftsman. So you can spend many a pleasant afternoon as you are taken round various houses to examine mini collections. Quality art is also sold in the street and parks, e.g. metal work, jewelry and wood carvings. The best places still to buy gifts and souvenirs are the 'salons,' the official handicraft galleries.
ANTIQUITIES — Remember that it is illegal to take out of the country any Uzbek antiquities unless accompanied by the relevant paperwork.

boots	**etik**
soleless leather boots	**mahsi**
box	**karobka; quti**
bracelet	**bilaguzuk**
brooch	**broshka**
candlestick	**shamdon**
carpet	**gilam**
chain	**zanjir**
clock	**soat**
copper	**mis**
crystal	**xrustal**
earrings	**zirak**
gold	**tillo; oltin**
handicraft	**qo'lhunar**
headscarf	**ro'mol**
iron	**temir**
jade	**klyacha**
jewelry	**zargarlik buyumlari; zirak-uzuk**
kilim	**palos**
leather	**teri**
metal	**metal**
modern	**zamonaviy**
necklace	**munchoq**
pottery	**sopol buyumlar**
ring	**uzuk**
rosary	**tasbeh**
silver	**kumush**
steel	**po'lat**
stone	**tosh**
traditional	**milliy; an'anaviy**
turban	**salla**
vase	**vaza**
watch	**soat**
wood	**yog'och**
wooden	**yog'ochdan yasalgan**

▬Clothes

bag	**sumka**
belt	**kamar**
boots	**etik**
cotton	**paxta(li)**
dress	**ko'ylak**
gloves	**qo'lqop**
handbag	**sumka**
hat	**shapka**
jacket	**kostyum**
jeans	**jinsi shim**
leather	**teri; kozha**
necktie	**galstuk**
overcoat	**plash**
pocket	**cho'ntak**
scarf	**sharf**
shirt	**ko'ylak**
shoes	**tufli**
socks	**noski**
suit	**kostyum-shim**
sweater	**jemper**
tights	**kolgotka**
trousers	**shim**
umbrella	**zontik**
underwear	**ishton/ichki kiyim**
uniform	**forma**
wool	**jun**

Traditional clothing . . .

The traditional clothing and fabrics of Uzbekistan are still very much in evidence, particularly at the many folk festivals dotted throughout the year. The basic outfit is as follows:

coat	**chopon**
silk material	**atlas**
silk dress	**atlas ko'ylak**
skullcap	**do'ppi**
headscarf	**ro'mol**

—Toiletries

aspirin	**aspirin**
Band-Aid	**leykoplastir**
comb	**taroq**
condom	**prezervativ**
cotton wool	**paxta**
deodorant	**dezodorant**
hairbrush	**soch cho'tkasi**
lipstick	**pomada**
mascara	**surma**
mouthwash	**og'iz chayish uchun suv**
nail-clippers	**tirnoq oladigan**
painkillers	**og'riq qoldiradigan dorilar**
perfume	**atir**
powder	**upa**
razor	**britva**
razorblade	**lezvie**
safety pin	**to'g'nog'ich**
shampoo	**shampun**
shaving cream	**soqol olish uchun krem**
sleeping pills	**uyqi dori**
soap	**sovun**
sponge	**gubka**
sunblock cream	**quyoshdan saqlanish uchun krem**
tampon	**tampon**
thermometer	**termometer**
tissues	**salfetka**
toilet paper	**xo'jalik qog'ozi**
toothbrush	**tish cho'tkasi**
toothpaste	**tish pastasi**

▬Stationery

ballpoint pen	**sharikli ruchka**
book	**kitob**
dictionary	**lug'at**
envelope	**konvert**
guidebook	**ma'lumotnoma; spravochnik**
ink	**siyoh**
magazine	**jurnal**
map	**xarita; karta**
road map	**yo'l xaritasi; yo'l kartasi**
a map of Tashkent	**Toshkent xaritasi**
newspaper	**gazeta**
newspaper in English	**inglizcha gazeta**
notebook	**daftar**
novel	**roman**
novels in English	**inglizcha yozilgan romanlar**
paper	**qog'oz**
a piece of paper	**bir varaq qog'oz**
pen	**ruchka**
pencil	**qalam**
postcard	**otkritka**
scissors	**qaychi**
writing paper	**(yozish uchun) qog'oz**

Do you have any foreign publications?	**Chet elda chiqadigan gazeta/jurnal bormi?**

▬Photography

How much is it to process (and print) this film?	**Bu plyonkani yuvib chiqarish qancha bo'ladi?**
When will it be ready?	**Qachon chiqadi?**

SHOPPING

I'd like film for this camera.	**Shu fotoapparat uchun plyonka olmoqchiman.**
B&W (film)	**oq-qora plyonka**
camera	**fotoapparat**
color (film)	**rangli plyonka**
film	**plyonka**
flash	**vspishka**
lens	**linza**
light meter	**yorug'lik o'lchaydigan apparat**

—Smoking

Cigarettes are usually purchased from kiosks. American brands are more pricy but still a bargain by western standards. The best value is to buy by the carton where prices are normally fixed. Uzbeks will smoke anywhere – it is rare indeed to find a smoke-free area and it is advisable to avoid constricted enclosed places if smoking creates problems for your health or if you simply find it offensive.

A pack of cigarettes, please.	**Bir pachka sigaret.**
Are these cigarettes strong?	**Bu sigaretlar kuchlimi?**
Do you have a light?	**Gugurtingiz bormi?**
Do you have any American cigarettes?	**Amerikaning sigaretlari bormi?**
cigar	**sigara**
cigarette(s)	**sigaret**
cigarette papers	**maxorka qog'ozi**
a carton of cigarettes	**bir karton sigaret**
filtered	**filtrli**
filterless	**filtrsiz**
flint	**chaqmoq tosh**

lighter	**chaqmoq; zajigalka**
matches	**gugurt**
menthol	**yalpiz hidli**
pipe	**trubka**
tobacco	**tamaki**

—Electrical equipment

adapter	**adaptor**
battery	**batareya**
cassette	**kasseta**
CD	**sidi**
CD player	**sidi pleyer**
fan	**ventilyator**
hairdryer	**fen; soch quritadigan**
heating coil	**suv qaynatadigan; kipyatilnik**
iron (for clothing)	**dazmol**
kettle	**choygun**
plug	**rozetka**
portable tv	**ko'tarib yuradigan televizor**
radio	**radio**
record	**plastinka**
tape (cassette)	**kasseta**
tape recorder	**magnitofon**
television	**televizor**
transformer	**transformator**
video (player)	**videomagnitofon**
videotape	**videokasseta**

—Sizes

small		**kichik (razmer)**
big		**katta (razmer)**
heavy	*weight*	**og'ir**
	material	**qalin**

light	**yengil**
more	**ko'proq**
less	**kamroq**
many	**ko'p**
too much/many	**juda ko'p**
enough	**yetarli**
That's enough.	**Bo'ldi.**
also	**yana**
a little bit	**ozgina**
Do you have a carrier bag?	**Sizda katta sumka bormi?**

Shops and markets . . .

WHEN TO SHOP — Shops open around 9am and close around 7pm. New private shops tend not to break for lunch, while older state shops do. Markets are open every day.

HOW TO PAY — Everything is best paid for in cash. Credit cards are increasingly acceptable in the cities but travelers' checks are still difficult to cash. Many shops now have price tags attached to items but in most places you will have to ask.

FOOD AND WINE — As well as the main streets of stores in the town centers, every street seems to have its own small produce kiosk or store. There is also a growing number of specialty shops, including supermarkets where you can buy western products.

MARKETS — For fresh produce go to a bazaar or **market**, where prices and availability of goods are seasonal. As a foreigner, you may occasionally find yourself paying a little more here – but not much! The best time is early morning when everything is at its freshest, particularly for meat. In the evenings you'll get a better price (Uzbeks call this **kechki bozor**), but less choice. Many local delicacies can be found here, including all kinds of fruit, smoked and dried meats, and a veritable plethora of spices, nuts and fruit. In Tashkent, visit the colorful flower markets or the **talkuchka** – markets where you can buy all the usual consumer products at a bargain, from cigarettes to CD-players, from clothing to pirate videos.

11. WHAT'S TO SEE

Do you have a guide-
book/local map?

**Shu yerning xaritasi/
ma'lumotnomasi
(spravochnigi) bormi?**

Is there a guide who
speaks English?

**Inglizcha biladigan
gid bormi?**

What are the main
attractions?

**Tomosha qilsa
bo'ladigan joylar
qaysilari?**

What is that?

Ana u nima?

How old is it?

Eskimi?

May I take a photograph?

**Rasmga olsam
maylimi?**

What time does it open?

Qachon ochiladi?

What time does it close?

Qachon yopiladi?

What is this monument/
statue?

**Bu yodgorlik/haykal
nima?**

What does that say?

**U yerda nima
yozilgan?**

Who is that statue of?

Bu kimning haykali?

Is there an entrance fee?

Kirish pullimi?

How much?

Necha pul?

Are there any night clubs/
discos?

Diskotekalar bormi?

Where can I hear local
folk music?

**Xalq muzikasini
qayerda eshitsa
bo'ladi?**

How much does it cost to
get in?

**Kirish uchun qancha
to'lash kerak?**

What's there to do in
the evening?

**Kechki payt nima
qilsa bo'ladi?**

WHAT'S TO SEE

Is there a concert?	**Kontsert bormi?**
When is the wedding?	**To'y qachon?**
What time does it begin?	**Qachon boshlanadi?**
Can we swim here?	**Bu yerda suzsa bo'ladimi?**

—Events

ballet	**balet**
blues	**blyuz**
classical music	**klassik muzika**
dancing	**raqs(ga tushish)**
disco	**diskoteka**
disk jockey	**disk jokey**
elevator	**lift**
escalator	**eskalator**
exhibition	**ko'rgazma**
folk dancing	**xalq o'yinlari**
folk music	**xalq muzikasi**
jazz	**jaz**
lift	**lift**
nightclub	**klub**
opera	**opera**
party	**o'tirish**
pop music	**estrada**
pub	**pivoxona; bar**
rock concert	**rok kontserti**
rock 'n' roll	**rok muzikasi**

—Buildings

academy of sciences	**fanlar akademiyasi**
apartment	**kvartira**
apartment building	**do'm**
archaeological	**arxeologik**
art gallery	**san'at ko'rgazmasi**
bakery	**non do'koni**
bar	**bar**

apartment block	**do'm**
building	**bino**
casino	**kazino**
castle	**qal'a**
cemetery	**qabriston**
church	**cherkov**
cinema	**kinoteatr**
city map	**shahar xaritasi**
college	**universitet**
concert	**konsert**
concert hall	**konsert zali**
embassy	**elchixona**
hospital	**bolnitsa; kasalxona**
house	**uy**
housing estate/project	**kvartal**
library	**kutubxona**
main square	**skver**
market	**bozor**
monument	**yodgorlik**
mosque	**machit**
museum	**muzey**
old city	**eski shahar**
opera house	**opera zali**
park	**park; bog'**
parliament (building)	**parlament binosi**
restaurant	**restoran; oshxona**
ruins	**xaroba(lar)**
saint's tomb	**ziyoratgoh**
'salon' shop	**salon-magazin**
school	**maktab**
shop	**do'kon**
shrine	**ziyoratgoh**
stadium	**stadion**
statue	**haykal**
synagogue	**senago'g**
temple	**ibodatxona**
theater	**teatr**

tomb	**go'r**
tower	**minora**
university	**universitet**
zoo	**hayvonot bog'i**

▬Occasions

birth	**tug'ilish**
death	**vafot**
funeral	**janoza**
marriage	**turmush qurish**
wedding ceremony	**nikoh to'yi**
circumcision ceremony	**sunnat to'yi**

Religious heritage . . .

The overwhelming majority of the population of Uzbekistan is Sunni Muslim. Additionally, there are also members of the Russian Orthodox Church and ever-dwindling numbers of Jews. Aside from mosques, you will also discover the odd synagogue or church. Mosques and madrasas (religious schools) have always played an important part in the development of the Uzbek people and state, and, although the Soviet period and now the demands of modern times have greatly undermined its power and influence, Islam still makes its presence felt through the often stunning religious buildings still standing throughout the country. Of particular significance are the monuments in Samarqand, Bukhara, and Khiva, but there are historic buildings wherever you look in Uzbekistan.

HOLIDAYS & FESTIVALS — There are a wide variety of traditional festivals celebrated in every village and area. Important dates in the national calendar are **Ramazon** (Ramadan, the month of fasting), **Ro'za hayiti** (Id al-Fitr, when the end of Ramadan and fasting is celebrated), **Qurbon hayiti** (Hajj holiday), and **Navruz Bayrami** — the Persian New Year or Spring Festival (March 21st). Because of the influence of European and Russian (Soviet) tradition, New Year (December 31st/January 1st) celebrations have also become one of the major festivities.

12. FINANCE

CURRENCIES — The official currency in Uzbekistan is the **som**, divided into 100 **tiyin**. Unofficially in use, but still accepted everywhere outside of government establishments and retail outlets, are U.S. dollars. These may be refused however if notes are creased, torn, old, or simply a low denomination. Be prepared to accept change in **som**.

CHANGING MONEY — Aside from the banks, money can also be changed in any bureau de change, where you will find reliable, up-to-date exchange rates prominently displayed on a board. The cashiers will often know a European language or two, and almost all will show the workings of the exchange on a calculator for you and give you a receipt. Many shops and kiosks will also be happy to change money for you.

I want to change some dollars.	**Dollar almashtirmoqchiman.**
I want to change some euros.	**Yuro almashtirmoqchiman.**
I want to change some pounds.	**Funt almashtirmoqchiman.**
Where can I change some money?	**Qayerda pul almashtirsam bo'ladi?**
What is the exchange rate?	**Kurs qancha?**
What is the commission?	**Qancha op qolinadi?**
Could you please check that again?	**Qaytadan hisoblab ko'rolasizmi?**
Could you write that down for me?	**Yozib berolasizmi?**
dollar	**dollar**
euro	**yuro**
ruble	**rubl**
pound sterling	**funt sterling**

FINANCE

bank notes	**banknot**
calculator	**kalkulyator**
cashier	**kassir**
coins	**tanga**
credit card	**kredit kartochkasi**
commission	**foiz**
exchange	**pul almashtirish punkti**
loose change	**mayda (pul)**
receipt	**kvitansiya**
signature	**imzo**

Courtesy . . .

Uzbeks pride themselves on being a courteous people and this is reflected in the expressions they use towards guests and superiors. Some related expressions you'll commonly hear are:

Khush kelibsiz!	Welcome (to our home)! *This is said after you have entered a house, sat down, exchanged greetings, drunk tea, etc.*
Marhamat!	Welcome! *or* Please . . . !
Eshigimiz doimo ochiq!	Our door is always open for you!
Tez-tez kelib turinglar!	Come again and again!

13. COMMUNICATIONS

TELECOMMUNICATIONS — All local calls are free, although you need to use tokens (**jeto'n**) in public phones. International calls are dialed direct, or else booked through the international operator – this may incur a wait of several hours. Phones give one long ring to indicate a local call, two shorter rings for an international call. Satellite telephone links are costly but are a reliable and secure method of communication. Pagers and mobile phones are widely used (including GSM). Mobile phones may be rented for a period of time.

Where is the post office?	**Pochta qayoqda?**
What time does the post office open?	**Pochta qachon ochiladi?**
What time does the post office close?	**Pochta qachon yopiladi?**
Where is the mail box?	**Pochta yashigi qayerda?**
Is there any mail for me?	**Menga xat bormi?**
How long will it take for this to get there?	**Qachon yetib boradi?**
How much does it cost to send this to . . . ?	**Mana buni . . .-ga yuborish qancha turadi?**
I would like some stamps.	**Marka olmoqchiman.**
I would like to send . . .	**. . . yubormoqchiman.**
a letter	**xat**
a postcard	**otkritka**
a parcel	**posilka**
a telegram	**telegramma**
air mail	**aviaxat**
envelope	**konvert**

COMMUNICATIONS

mailbox	**pochta qutisi/yashigi**
packet	**posilka**
registered mail	**zakaz xat**
stamp	**marka**
telegram	**telegramma**
postal wrapper	**banderol**

—Tele-etiquette

I would like to make a phone call.	**Telefon qilmoqchiman.**
I would like to send a fax.	**Faks yubormoqchiman.**
I would like to send a telex.	**Teleks yubormoqchiman.**
Where is the telephone?	**Telefon qayerda?**
May I use your phone?	**Telefoningizni ishlatsam maylimi?**
Can I telephone from here?	**Shu yerdan telefon qilsam bo'ladimi?**
Can you help me get this number?	**Shu nomerga telefon qilishga yordam berolasizmi?**
Can I dial direct?	**To'g'ri telefon qilsa bo'ladimi?**
May I speak to . . . ?	**. . . bilan gaplashmoqchiman.**
Can I leave a message?	**Mening aytadigan gaplarimni yozib berolasizmi?**
Who is calling, please?	**Kim telefon qilyapti?**
Who are you calling?	**Kimga telefon qilyapsiz?**
Can I take your name?	**Ismingizni yozib olsam maylimi?**
Which number are you dialing?	**Qaysi nomerga telefon qilyapsiz?**

He/She is not here at the moment, would you like to leave a message?	**Hozir yo'q, nima deb qo'yay?**
This is not . . . You are mistaken.	**Bu . . . emas. Boshqa joyga tushdingiz.**
This is the . . . office.	**Bu yer . . . ofisi.**
Hello, I need to speak to . . .	**Assalamu alaykum, . . . bilan gaplashmoqchi edim.**
I am calling this number . . .	**Men . . .-ga telefon qilmoqchiman.**
The telephone is switched off.	**Telefon ishlamayapti.**
I want to call . . .	**. . .-ga telefon qilmoqchiman.**
What is the code for . . . ?	**. . . ning kodi necha?**
What is the international code?	**Xalqaro telefon kodi necha?**
The number is . . .	**(Uning nomeri) . . .**
The extension is . . .	**Ilova nomeri . . .**
It's busy.	**Band.**
I've been cut off.	**Uzildi.**
The lines have been cut.	**Simlar uzilgan.**
Where is the nearest public phone?	**Eng yaqin telefon-avtomat qayoqda?**
digital	**digital**
e-mail	**elektron pochta**
fax	**faks**
fax machine	**faks apparati**
handset	**trubka**
international operator	**xalqaro telegrafist**
Internet	**internet**
line	**xat**

mobile phone	**uyali/sotoviy telefon**
modem	**modem**
operator	**telegrafist(ka)**
satellite phone	**sputnik telefoni**
telephone center	**telefon stantsiyasi**
telex	**teleks**
to transfer/put through	**ula-**

—Faxing & e-mailing

Where can I send a fax from?	**Qayerdan faks jo'natsam bo'ladi?**
Can I fax from here?	**Shu yerdan faks jo'natsam bo'ladimi?**
How much is it to fax?	**Faks jo'natish qancha turadi?**
Where can I find a place to e-mail from?	**Qayerdan elektron pochta yozib yuborish mumkin?**
Is there an internet cafe near here?	**Bu yerga yaqin internet joyi bormi?**
Can I e-mail from here?	**Shu yerdan email jo'natish mumkinmi?**
How much is it to use a computer?	**Kompyuterlarni ishlatish qancha turadi?**
How do you turn on this computer?	**Bu kompyuterni qanaqa yoqish kerak?**
The computer has crashed.	**Kompyuter to'xtab qoldi.**
I need help with this computer.	**Bu kompyuterni ishlatish uchun menga yordam kerak.**
I don't know how to use this program.	**Bu programmani bilmayman.**
I know how to use this program.	**Bu programmani bilaman.**
I want to print.	**Printerdan nusxa chiqarmoqchiman.**

14. THE OFFICE

chair	**stul**
computer	**kompyuter**
desk	**stol**
drawer	**tortma**
fax	**faks**
file *paper*	**kartoteka**
computer	**fayl**
meeting	**majlis**
paper	**qog'oz**
pen	**ruchka**
pencil	**qalam**
photocopier	**kseroks mashinasi**
photocopy	**kseroks**
printer	**printer**
program (computer)	**programma**
red tape	**qog'ozbozlik**
report	**hisobot**
ruler	**lineyka**
telephone	**telefon**
telex	**teleks**
typewriter	**mashinka**

15. THE CONFERENCE

article	**maqola**
a break for refreshments	**dam olish uchun tanaffus**
conference room	**konferentsiya zali**
copy	**kopiya**
discussion	**mulohaza**
forum	**forum**
guest speaker	**mehmon notiq**
a paper	**maqola**
podium	**podium**
projector	**proyektor**
session	**sessiya**
a session chaired by . . .	**. . . boshchilik qilgan sessiya**
speaker	**notiq**
subject	**mavzu**

Yes & no . . .

YES – The word for yes, **ha**, is used more like 'uh-huh'; perhaps a more accurate way of saying yes is to simply repeat the main verb in the question, e.g. **"Shu yerda telefon bormi?"** "Is there a telephone here?" **"Bor."** "There is." – or, more simply, **"Bormi?"** "Is there any?" **"Bor."** "There is."

NO – Saying **yo'q** directly can be a little rude. As above with 'yes', one usually repeats the key element of the question, e.g. **"Yo'q, bormayman."** "No, I'm not going."

16. AGRICULTURE

agriculture	**dehqonchilik**
barley	**arpa**
barn	**og'il**
cattle	**qoramol**
to clear land	**yer och-**
combine harvester	**kombayn**
corn	**makka (jo'xori)**
cotton	**paxta**
crops	**ekin(lar)**
earth	**tuproq**
fallowland	**bo'sh qolgan dala**
farm	**ferma**
farmer	**fermer; dehqon**
farming	**dehqonchilik**
(animal) feed	**yem**
fertilizer	**o'g'it**
field	**dala**
fruit	**meva**
garden	**tomorqa**
to grow crops	**ekin ek-**
harvest	**hosil**
hay	**xashak**
haystack	**g'aram**
irrigation	**sug'orish**
marsh	**botqoq**
mill	**tegirmon**
orchard *apple orchard*	**olmazor**
mulberry orchard	**tutzor**
peach orchard	**shaftolizor**
planting	**ekin ekish**
plow	**plug**
to plow	**yer hayda-**
reaping	**o'rim**

AGRICULTURE

rice (plant)	**sholi**
rice (as grain)	**guruch**
season	**mavsum**
seed	**urug'**
silkworm	**ipak qurti**
to sow	**urug' ek-**
tractor	**traktor**
wheat	**bug'doy**
well (of water)	**quduq**

17. ANIMALS

—Mammals

bear		ayiq
bull		buqa
camel		tuya
cat		mushuk
cow		sigir
deer		kiyik
dog		kuchuk; it
donkey		eshak
fish		baliq
flock	*sheep*	to'da
	birds	gala
goat		echki
herd		poda
horse		ot
lamb		qo'zi
mare		baytal
mouse		sichqon
mule		xachir
pig		cho'chqa
pigeon		kaptar
pony		toychoq
rabbit		quyon
ram		qo'chqor
rat		kalamush
sheep		qo'y
sheepdog		cho'pon iti
stallion		ayg'ir
wolf		bo'ri

—Birds

bird	qush
chicken; hen	tovuq

ANIMALS

crow	**qarg'a**
duck	**o'rdak**
eagle	**burgut**
goose	**g'oz**
owl	**boyo'g'li**
partridge	**kaklik**
rooster	**xo'roz**
turkey	**induk**

—Insects & amphibians

ant	**chumoli**
bee	**asalari**
butterfly	**kapalak**
caterpillar	**qurt**
cockroach	**suvarak; tarakan**
fish	**baliq**
flea	**burga**
fleas	** burgalar**
fly	**pashsha**
frog	**qurbaqa**
insect	**hasharot**
lice	**bit**
lizard	**kaltakesak**
mosquito	**chivin**
snail	**shilliqqurt**
snake	**ilon**
spider	**o'rgimchak**
termite	**termit**
tick	**kana**
wasp	**ari**
worm	**chuvalchang**

18. COUNTRYSIDE

avalanche	**lavina; qor ko'chkisi**
canal	**kanal**
cave	**g'or**
dam	**to'g'on**
earthquake	**zilzila**
fire	**yong'in**
flood	**sel**
foothills	**adir**
footpath	**so'qmoq; yo'l**
forest	**o'rmon**
hill	**tepa(lik)**
lake	**ko'l**
landslide	**tog' ko'chkisi**
mountain	**tog'**
mountain pass	**dovon; pereval**
peak	**cho'qqi**
plain	**dala**
plant	**o'simlik**
range	**o'tloq**
ravine	**soy**
river	**daryo**
river bank	**qirg'oq**
rock	**tosh**
slope	**qiyalik**
stream	**daryocha**
summit	**cho'qqi**
swamp	**botqoq**
tree	**daraxt**
valley	**soy; vodiy**
waterfall	**shalola**
a wood	**daraxtzor**

19. THE WEATHER

Most of Uzbekistan comprises mid-latitude desert, though in the Ferghana Valley and other eastern regions you'll find cooler and more forested foothills. Summers can be very hot with temperatures over 40°C, but winters are mostly mild. Uzbekistan has all four seasons, with quite mild and pleasant weather in the spring and fall, much like any other temperate country.

What's the weather like?	**Havo qanday?**
The weather is . . . today.	**Bugun havo . . .**
cold	**sovuq**
cool; fresh	**salqin**
cloudy	**bulut**
foggy	**tuman tushgan**
freezing	**muzday sovuq; muzlayapti**
hot	**issiq**
misty	**tumanli**
very hot	**juda issiq**
windy	**shamol esyapti**

It's going to rain.	**Yomg'ir yog'adi shekilli.**
It is raining.	**Yomg'ir yog'yapti.**
It's going to snow.	**Qor yog'adi shekilli.**
It is snowing.	**Qor yog'yapti.**
It is sunny.	**Quyosh chiqdi.**

air	**havo**
cloud	**bulut**
fog	**tuman**
frost	**qirov**
full moon	**to'lin oy**

THE WEATHER

heatwave	**juda issiq payt**
ice	**muz**
midsummer	**yoz chillasi**
midwinter	**qish chillasi**
moon	**oy**
new moon	**yangi tug'ilgan oy**
rain	**yomg'ir**
severe winter	**qahraton qish**
sleet	**do'l**
snow	**qor**
solstice	**quyosh turishi**
star	**yulduz**
sun	**quyosh**
sunny	**quyoshli**
thaw	**qor eriydigan vaqt**
weather	**ob-havo**

—Seasons

spring	**bahor**
summer	**yoz**
autumn	**kuz**
winter	**qish**

20. CAMPING

This is not a popular pastime among Uzbeks. (Daily life provides enough hardships.) It is not uncommon for Uzbeks to take family outings, though, such as to the mountains. Chimyon is a popular spot outside of Tashkent.

Where can we camp?	**Qayerda chodir tiksak bo'ladi?**
Can we camp here?	**Shu yerda chodir qurish bo'ladimi?**
Is it safe to camp here?	**Shu yerda chodir qurish xavflimi?**
Is there drinking water?	**Ichiladigan suv bormi?**
May we light a fire?	**O't yoqsak bo'ladimi?**

axe	**bolta**
backpack	**ryuksak**
bucket	**chelak**
campsite	**chodir tikiladigan joy**
can opener	**banka ochadigan**
compass	**kompas**
firewood	**o'tin**
flashlight	**qo'l fonari**
gas canister	**gaz baloni**
hammer	**bolg'a**
ice axe/pick	**al'pinistlar boltasi**
lamp	**chiroq**
mattress	**matras**
penknife	**pakki; qalamtarosh**
rope	**arqon**
sleeping bag	**spalniy mesho'k**
stove	**plita**
tent	**chodir**
tent pegs	**qoziqlar**
water bottle	**su shisha; butilka**

21. EMERGENCY

COMPLAINING — If you really feel you have been cheated or misled, raise the matter first with your host or the proprietor of the establishment in question preferably with a smile. Uzbeks are proud but courteous, with a deeply felt tradition of hospitality, and consider it their duty to help any guest. Angry glares and shouting will get you nowhere.

CRIME — Uzbeks are law-abiding people, but petty theft does occur. Without undue paranoia, take usual precautions: watch your wallet or purse, securely lock your equipment and baggage before handing it over to railway or airline porters, and don't leave valuables on display in your hotel room. On buses, look out for pickpockets – keep valuables in front pockets and your bag close to your side. If you are robbed, contact the police. Of course in the more remote areas, sensible precautions should be taken, and always ensure that you go with a guide. In general, follow the same rules as you would in your own country and you will run little risk of encountering crime.

LOST ITEMS — If you lose something, save time and energy by appealing only to senior members of staff or officials. If you have lost items in the street or left anything in public transport, the police may be able to help.

DISABLED FACILITIES — The terrain and conditions throughout most of Uzbekistan do not make it easy for any visitor to get around in a wheelchair even at the best of times. Access to most buildings in the cities is difficult, particularly since the majority of lifts function irregularly. Facilities are rarely available in hotels, airports or other public areas.

TOILETS — You will find public utilities located in any important or official building. You may use those in hotels or restaurants. You may sometimes encounter failed plumbing and absence of toilet paper. Similar to Turkey and countries in the Middle East, people in Uzbekistan tend to use any available paper as toilet paper, and occasionally a jug of water (rural areas).

wheelchair	**nogironlar aravachasi**
disabled	**nogiron**
Do you have seats for the disabled?	**Nogironlar uchun joy bormi?**
Do you have access for the disabled?	**Nogironlar uchun sharoitlar bormi?**

Do you have facilities for the disabled?	**Nogironlar uchun sharoitlar bormi?**
Help!	**Dod!** or **Yordam beringlar!**
Could you help me, please?	**Menga yordam berolasizmi?**
Do you have a telephone?	**Telefon bormi?**
Where is the nearest telephone?	**Eng yaqin telefon qayoqda?**
Does the phone work?	**Bu telefon ishlaydimi?**
Get help quickly!	**Tezroq yordam beroladigan odamlarni opkeling!**
Call the police.	**Militsiyani chaqiring.**
I'll call the police!	**Militsiyani chaqiraman!**
Is there a doctor near here?	**Shu yerda doktor bormi?**
Call a doctor.	**Doktorga telefon qiling.**
Call an ambulance.	**Tez yordamni chaqiring.**
I'll get medical help!	**Tez yordam chaqiraman!**
Where is the doctor?	**Doktor qani?**
Where is a doctor?	**Qayerda doktor bor?**
Where is the hospital?	**Bolnitsa qayerda?**
Where is the pharmacy?	**Apteka qayoqda?**
Where is the dentist?	**Tish doktori qayerda bor?**
Where is the police station?	**Militsiya uchastkasi qayerda?**
Take me to a doctor.	**Meni bitta doktorga oboring.**
There's been an accident.	**Avariya bo'ldi.**
Is anyone hurt?	**Yaralanganlar bormi?**

This person is hurt.	**Bu kishi yaralanipti.**
There are people injured.	**Yaralanganlar bor.**
Don't move!	**Qimirlamang!**
Go away!	**Boring! Keting!**
Stand back!	**Uzoq turing!**
I am lost.	**Men adashib qoldim.**
I am ill.	**Mazam yo'q.**
I've been raped.	**Meni bittasi zo'rladi.**
I've been robbed.	**Pulimni o'g'irlatdim.**
Stop, thief!	**O'g'rini ushlanglar!**
My . . . has been stolen.	**. . .-imni o'g'irlatdim.**
I have lost . . .	**. . .-ni yo'qotdim.**
my bags	**sumkalarimni;**
	chamadonlarimni
my camera equipment	**fotoapparat**
	jihozlarimni
my handbag	**sumkamni**
my laptop computer	**laptop**
	kompyuterimni
my money	**pulimni**
my passport	**pasportimni**
my sound equipment	**magnitofon**
	jihozlarimni
my traveler's checks	**sayohat**
	cheklarimni
my wallet	**bumazhnigimni**
My possessions are	**Narsalarim sug'urta**
insured.	**qilingan.**
I have a problem.	**Menga yordam kerak.**
I didn't do it.	**Men qilmadim.**
I'm sorry.	**Kechirasiz.**
I apologize.	**Uzr.**
I didn't realize anything	**Hech nimani**
was wrong.	**payqamadim.**

EMERGENCY

I want to contact my embassy.	**Elchixonaga telefon qilmoqchiman.**
I speak English.	**Inglizcha bilaman.**
I need an interpreter.	**Menga tarjumon kerak.**
Where are the toilets?	**Tualetlar qayerda?**

Weights & measures . . .

Uzbekistan uses the metric system. For reference translations are also included for the most common imperial units (marked with an asterisk):

kilometer	**kilometr**
meter	**metr**
mile*	**mil**
foot*	**qadam**
yard*	**yard**
gallon*	**galon**
liter	**litr**
kilogram	**kilo**
gram	**gram**
pound*	**funt**
ounce*	**unts**

22. HEALTHCARE

INSURANCE — Make sure any insurance policy you take out covers Uzbekistan, although this will only help in flying you out in case of a serious accident or illness. No vaccinations are required for Uzbekistan, although your doctor may suggest you take the boosters usually recommended when making any trip outside of North America and Western Europe.
PHARMACIES — These are easy to find but can be understocked at times. If planning to travel off the beaten track, it is probably best to bring a sufficient supply of any specific medication you require. But most of the familiar range of medicines can be found in the capital, Tashkent. Don't forget to check the "best before" date.

What's the trouble?	**Nima bo'ldi?**
I am sick.	**Kasal bo'p qoldim.**
My companion is sick.	**O'rtog'im kasal.**
May I see a female doctor?	**Ayol doktor bilan ko'rishsam bo'ladimi?**
I have medical insurance.	**Tibbiy sug'urtam bor.**
Please undress.	**Yechining.**
How long have you had this problem?	**Qachondan beri shu naqa bo'lyapti?**
How long have you been feeling sick?	**Qachondan beri kasalsiz?**
Where does it hurt?	**Qayeringiz og'riyapti?**
It hurts here.	**Shu yerim og'riyapti.**
I have been vomiting.	**Qusyapman.**
I feel dizzy.	**Boshim aylanyapti.**
I can't eat.	**Ovqat yeyolmayapman.**
I can't sleep.	**Uxlayolmayapman.**
I feel worse.	**Yomonroq his qilyapman.**

I feel better.	**Tuzalib qoldim.**
Do you have diabetes?	**Qand kasalimisiz?**
Do you have epilepsy?	**Tutqanog'ingiz bormi?**
Do you have asthma?	**Astmangiz bormi?**
I'm pregnant.	**Homiladorman.**
I have . . .	
a cold.	**Shammollab qoldim.**
a cough.	**Yo'talyapman.**
a headache.	**Boshim og'riyapti.**
a pain (in my . . .).	**. . .-im og'riyapti.**
a sore throat.	**Tomog'im og'riyapti.**
a temperature.	**Isitmam chiqyapti.**
an allergy.	**Allergiyam bor.**
an infection.	**. . .-im yiringlab ketdi.**
an itch.	**. . .-im qichishyapti.**
backache.	**Belim og'riyapti.**
constipation.	**Ichim qotib qoldi.**
diarrhea.	**Ichim ketyapti.**
a fever.	**Isitmam chiqyapti.**
hepatitis.	**Sariq kasalman.**
indigestion.	**Qornim og'riyapti.**
influenza.	**Gripman.**
a heart condition.	**Yuragim yomon.**
pins and needles.	**Qo'l-oyog'im uvishib qoldi.**
stomachache.	**Qornim og'riyapti.**
a fracture.	**. . .-m darz ketdi.**
toothache.	**Tishim og'riyapti.**
You have . . .	
a cold.	**Shamollagansiz.**
a cough.	**Yo'talyapsiz.**
a headache.	**Boshingiz og'riyapti.**
a pain.	**Og'riq sezyapsiz.**
a sore throat.	**Tomog'ingiz og'riyapti.**
a temperature.	**Issig'ingiz chiqyapti.**

an allergy.	**Allergiyangiz bor.**
an infection.	**. . .-ingiz yiringlagan.**
an itch.	**. . .-ingiz qichishyapti.**
backache.	**Belingiz og'riyapti.**
constipation.	**Ichingiz qotib qoldi.**
diarrhea.	**Ichingiz ketyapti.**
a fever.	**Isitmangiz chiqyapti.**
hepatitis.	**Sariq kasalsiz.**
indigestion.	**Me'dangiz buzilyapti.**
influenza.	**Gripsiz.**
a heart condition.	**Yurak kasalligingiz bor.**
pins and needles.	**Qo'l-oyog'ingiz uvishib qoldi.**
stomachache.	**Qorningiz og'riyapti.**
a fracture.	**. . .-ngiz darz ketdi.**
toothache.	**Tishingiz og'riyapti.**

I take this medication.	**Shu dorini iching.**
I need medication for . . .	**Menga . . . uchun dori kerak.**
What type of medication is this?	**Bu qanaqa dori?**
How many times a day must I take it?	**Bir kunda necha marta ichish kerak?**
When should I stop?	**Qachon to'xtashim kerak?**

I'm on antibiotics.	**Men antibiotik ichyapman.**
I'm allergic to . . .	**Mening . . .-ga ailerigiyam bor.**
antibiotics	**antibiotik**
penicillin	**penitsillin**
I have been vaccinated.	**Men emlanganman.**
I have my own syringe.	**O'z shpritsim bor.**

Is it possible for me to travel?	**Yo'lga chiqishim mumkinmi?**

—Health words

AIDS	**SPID**
alcoholic	**aroqxo'r**
alcoholism	**aroqxo'rlik**
altitude sickness	**balandlik kasalligi**
amputation	**amputatsiya**
anemia	**kamqonlik**
anesthetic	**og'riq qoldiruvchi**
anesthetist	**anesteziolog**
antibiotic	**antibiotik**
antiseptic	**antiseptik**
aspirin	**aspirin**
blood	**qon**
blood group	**qon gruppasi**
blood pressure:	**qon bosimi**
low blood pressure	**gipotoniya**
high blood pressure	**gipertoniya**
blood transfusion	**qon quyish**
bone	**suyak**
cancer	**rak**
cholera	**vabo**
clinic	**(poli)klinika**
dentist	**tish do'xtiri**
drug *medical*	**dori**
narcotic	**narkotik**
epidemic	**epidemiya**
fever	**isitma**
flu	**gripp**
frostbite	**sovuq oldirish**
germs	**mikrob**
heart attack	**infarkt**
hygiene	**gigiyena**

infection	**infektsiya**
limbs	**qo'l-oyoq**
needle	**ukol**
nurse	**hamshira**
operating theater	**operatsiya xonasi**
(surgical) operation	**operatsiya**
oxygen	**kislorod**
painkiller	**og'riq qoldiruvchi**
physiotherapy	**fizioterapiya**
rabies	**quturish**
shrapnel	**snaryad parchasi**
sleeping pill	**uyqu dorisi**
snake bite	**ilon chaqishi**
stethoscope	**stetoskop**
surgeon	**xirurg; jarroh**
(act of) surgery	**operatsiya**
syringe	**shprits**
thermometer	**termometr**
torture	**qiynoq**
tranquilizer	**tinchlantiruvchi**

I have broken my glasses.	**Ko'zoynagimni sindirib qo'ydim.**
Can you repair them?	**Tuzatib berolasizmi?**
I need new lenses.	**Menga yangi linza kerak.**
When will they be ready?	**Qachon tayyor bo'ladi?**
How much do I owe you?	**Qancha berishim kerak?**

contact lenses	**kontakt linza**
contact lens solution	**kontakt linza saqlanadigan suyuqlik**

23. RELIEF AID

Can you help me?	**Menga yordam berolasizmi?**
Do you speak English?	**Inglizcha bilasizmi?**
Who is in charge?	**Boshliq kim?**
Fetch the main person in charge.	**Boshlig'ingizni chaqiring.**
What's the name of this town?	**Bu yerning nomi nima?**
How many people live there?	**Bu yerning aholisi qancha?**
What's the name of that river?	**U daryoning nomi nima?**
How deep is it?	**Uning chuqurligi qancha?**
Is the bridge still standing?	**Ko'prik hali ham turibdimi?**
What is the name of that mountain?	**O'sha tog'ning nomi nima?**
How high is it?	**Balandligi qancha?**
Where is the border?	**Chegara qayerda?**
Is it safe?	**Xavfsizmi?**
Show me.	**Menga ko'rsating.**

—Checkpoints

checkpoint	**tekshiruv punkti**
roadblock	**post**
Stop!	**To'xta!**
Do not move!	**Qimirlama!**
Go!	**Yur!**
Who are you?	**Siz kimsiz?**
Don't shoot!	**Otmang!**
Help!	**Dod!**
	or **Yordam beringlar!**

RELIEF AID

no entry	**kirish mumkin emas**
emergency exit	**avariya holatida chiqish**
straight on	**to'g'riga**
turn left	**chapga buriling**
turn right	**o'ngga buriling**
this way	**shu yo'ldan;**
	shu tarafga
that way	**o'sha yo'ldan;**
	o'sha tarafga
Keep quiet!	**Jim!**
You are right.	**Gapingiz to'g'ri.**
	or **To'g'ri aytdingiz.**
You are wrong.	**Yo'q, gapingiz**
	noto'g'ri.
I am ready.	**Tayyorman.**
I am in a hurry.	**Shoshyapman.**
Well, thank you!	**Rahmat-e!**
What's that?	**Ana u nima?**
Come in!	**Keling!**
That's all!	**Bo'ldi!**

─Food distribution

feeding station	**ovqatlanish joyi**
How many people are in your family?	**Oilangizda nechtasizlar?**
How many children?	**Nechta bola bor?**
You must come back . . .	**. . . keling.**
this afternoon	**bugun obeddan keyin**
tonight	**kechasi**
tomorrow	**ertaga**
the day after tomorrow	**indinga**
next week	**keyingi hafta**
There is water for you.	**Sizga suv bor.**
There is grain for you.	**Sizga don bor.**

There is food for you.	**Sizga ovqat bor.**
There is fuel for you.	**Sizga yonilg'i bor.**

—Road repair

Is the road passable?	**Bu yo'ldan yursa bo'ladimi?**
Is the road blocked?	**Yo'l bekitilganmi?**
We are repairing the road.	**Yo'lni tuzatyapmiz.**
We are repairing the bridge.	**Ko'prikni tuzatyapmiz.**
We need . . .	**Bizga . . . kerak.**
wood	**yog'och**
rock	**tosh**
gravel	**shag'al**
sand	**qum**
fuel	**yonilg'i**

—Mines

mine *noun*	**mina**
mines	**minalar**
minefield	**minalashtirilgan joy**
to lay mines	**minalashtir-**
to hit a mine	**minani bos-**
to clear a mine	**minani zararsizlantir-**
mine detector	**mina detektori**
mine disposal	**mina tozalash**
Are there any mines near here?	**Shu atroflarda mina bormi?**
What type are they?	**Qanday mina ekan?**
anti-vehicle	**mashinalarga qarshi**
anti-personnel	**piyodalarga qarshi**
plastic	**plastmassa**
floating	**suzuvchi**
magnetic	**magnitli**

What size are they?	**Kattaligi qanday ekan?**
What color are they?	**Rangi qanaqa ekan?**
Are they marked?	**Belgisi bormi?**
How are they marked?	**Belgisi qanaqa?**
How many mines are there?	**Nechta mina bor ekan?**
When were they laid?	**Ular qachon yotqizilgan?**
Can you take me to the minefields?	**Meni minalashtirilgan joylarga oborolasizmi?**
Are there any booby traps near there?	**Tuzoqlar bormi?**
Are they made from grenades, high explosives or something else?	**Tuzoqlar granatalardan, yuksak darajali portlovchi moddalardan, yoki boshqa narslardan qilingan?**
Are they in a building?	**Ular bitta binoning ichidami?**
on tracks?	**reylslardami?**
on roads?	**yo'llardami?**
on bridges?	**ko'priklardami?**
or elsewhere?	**yo boshqa joylardami?**
Can you show me?	**Ko'rsatib berolasizmi?**

—Other words

airforce	**harbiy havo kuchlari**
ambulance	**tez yordam mashinasi**
armored car	**bronemashina**
army	**armiya**
artillery	**artillerya**
barbed wire	**tikanli sim**
bomb	**bomba**
bomber	**bombardirovkachi**
bullet	**o'q**

cannon		**pushka**
disaster		**ofat**
drought		**qurg'oqchilik**
earthquake		**zilzila**
famine		**ocharchilik**
fighter		**jangchi**
gun	*pistol*	**to'pponcha**
	rifle	**miltiq**
	cannon	**pushka**
machine gun		**pulemyot**
missile		**raketa**
missiles		**raketalar**
natural disaster		**tabiiy ofat**
navy		**dengiz floti**
nuclear power		**yadro quvvati**
nuclear power station		**yadro stantsiyasi**
officer		**ofitser**
parachute		**parashyut**
peace		**tinchlik**
people		**odamlar**
pistol		**to'pponcha; pistolet**
refugee		**qochoq**
refugees		**qochoqlar**
refugee camp		**qochoqlar lageri**
relief aid		**yordam**
sack		**qop**
shell		**snaryad**
submachine gun		**avtomat**
tank		**tank**
troops		**otryad; qo'shin**
unexploded bomb		**portlamagan bomba**
United Nations		**Birlashgan Millatlar Tashkiloti**
war		**urush**
weapon		**qurol**

24. TOOLS

binoculars	**durbin**
brick	**g'isht**
brush	**cho'tka**
cable	**kabel**
cooker	**plita**
drill	**parma**
eyeglasses	**ko'zoynak**
gas bottle	**gaz balloni**
hammer	**bolg'a**
handle	**dastak; ruchka**
hose	**shlang**
insecticide	**insektitsid**
ladder	**narvon; shoti**
machine	**mashina**
microscope	**mikrosko'p**
nail	**mix**
padlock	**qulf**
paint	**bo'yoq**
pickaxe	**qo'shbosh**
plank	**taxta**
plastic	**plastmassa**
rope	**arqon**
rubber	**rezina**
rust	**zang**
saw	**arra**
scissors	**qaychi**
screw	**vint**
screwdriver	**otvertka**
spade	**kurak**
spanner/wrench	**gayka klyuchi**
string	**ip**
sunglasses	**qora ko'zoynak**
telescope	**telesko'p**
varnish	**lak**
wire	**sim**

25. THE CAR

DRIVING — Unless you already know the country well, it is inadvisable to bring your own vehicle to Uzbekistan. If you do, you will need an international driver's license, car registration papers and insurance. Driving conditions vary. Normally roads are well signposted. But side roads might be without warning of roadworks and sometimes manholes are not closed properly. Street lighting is sporadic, and traffic lights, if they exist, rarely work — but when they do Uzbeks seem to take great pleasure in ignoring them especially when no police or other vehicle are in sight, as in late at night. So you better look out for those who like crossing on red lights and make sure the crossroad is clear. Certain areas have parking restrictions, although it is not always obvious where they are or what the restrictions are. Rather than book you, the police will simply remove the license plates of an illegally parked car. The unfortunate driver then has to discover which police unit or station is holding them, and negotiate a suitable fee for their return. But in general you may park your car where you wish, provided that you do not block traffic.

Where can I rent a car?	**Qayerda ijaraga mashina olish mumkin?**
Where can I rent a car with a driver?	**Qayerda shofyor bilan mashinani ijaraga olish mumkin?**
How much is it per day?	**Kuniga necha pul bo'ladi?**
How much is it per week?	**Haftasiga necha pul bo'ladi?**
Can I park here?	**Mashinamni shu yerga qo'ysam bo'ladimi?**
Are we on the right road for . . . ?	**. . .-ga to'g'ri ketyapmizmi?**
Where is the nearest gas station?	**Eng yaqin benzinkolonka qayerda?**

Fill the tank please.	**Bakni to'ldirib bering.**
normal/diesel	**benzin/dizel**
Check the oil/tires/ battery, please.	**Yog'ni/g'ildiraklarni/ akkumulyatorni tekshirib bering.**
I've broken down.	**Mashinam buzilib qoldi.**
I have a flat tire/puncture.	**G'ildirak teshilgan.**
The tire is flat.	**Ballonning yeli chiqib ketibdi.**
I have run out of gas.	**Benzin qolmadi.**
Our car is stuck.	**Mashinamiz yerga botib qoldi.**
There's something wrong with this car.	**Bu mashinaga nimadir bo'lgan.**
We need a mechanic.	**Bizga mexanink kerak.**
Where is the nearest garage?	**Eng yaqin garaj qayerda?**
Can you tow us?	**Bizni tortib ketolasizmi?**
Can you jumpstart the car (by pushing)?	**Mashinani itarishib yuborolasizmi?**
There's been an accident.	**Avariya bo'ldi.**
My car has been stolen.	**Mashinamni o'g'irlab ketishdi.**
Call the police.	**Militsiyaga telefon qiling.**
driver's license	**prava**
insurance policy	**sug'urta**
car papers	**mashinaning dokumentlari/hujjatlari**
car registration	**registratsiya**

THE CAR

—Car words

accelerator	**gaz pedali**
air	**yel**
anti-freeze	**antifriz**
battery	**akkumulyator**
bonnet/hood	**kapot**
boot/trunk	**bagaj joyi**
brake	**tormoz**
bumper	**amortizator; bamper**
car park; parking lot	**mashina to'xtash joyi**
clutch	**stsepleniye**
driver	**shofyor**
engine	**motor**
exhaust	**vixlop; ishlangan gaz**
fan belt	**ventilyator qayishi**
gear	**peredacha**
indicator light	**indikator chirog'i**
inner-tube	**ballon**
jack	**domkrat**
mechanic	**mexanik**
neutral drive	**neytral**
oil	**yog'**
oilcan	**yog' bankasi**
passenger	**yo'lovchi**
petrol	**benzin**
radiator	**radiator**
reverse *gear*	**orqaga yurish; zadniy xod**
seat	**o'rindiq**
spare tyre/tire	**zapas g'ildirak/shina**
speed	**tezlik**
steering wheel	**rul**
tank	**bak**
tyre/tire	**shina; pokrishka**
tow rope	**tros**
windscreen wipers	**old oynani artadigan**
windscreen/windshield	**old oyna**

26. SPORTS

Displays of physical strength are greatly prized in Uzbek
society. Wrestling and horse-racing are particularly favorite
traditional sports. If you're lucky, you may even witness
ko'pkari (Afghan "kuzbashi"), a game played on horseback
in rural areas. More recent sports adopted include judo and
other martial arts, basketball and, of course, soccer.

athletics	**atletika**
ball	**to'p**
basketball	**basketbol**
chess	**shahmat**
goal	**gol**
horse racing	**poyga**
horseback-riding	**ot minish**
match	**o'yin; match**
soccer match	**futbol matchi**
pitch	**maydon**
referee	**sudya; hakam**
rugby	**regbi**
skating	**konki uchish**
skiing	**chang'i uchish**
soccer	**futbol**
stadium	**stadion**
swimming	**suzish**
team	**komanda**
wrestling	**kurash**
Who won?	**Kim yutdi?**
What's the score?	**Hisob necha bo'ldi?**
Who scored?	**Kim gol urdi?**

27. THE BODY

ankle	to'piq
arm	qo'l
back	orqa
lower back	bel
upper back/shoulders	yelka
beard	soqol
blood	qon
body	badan
bone	suyak
bottom	keyin
breast/chest	ko'krak
chin	iyak
ear	quloq
elbow	tirsak
eye	ko'z
face	yuz
finger	barmoq
foot	oyoq
genitals	jinsiy a'zolar
hair *on head*	soch
on body	qil; tuk
hand	qo'l
head	bosh
heart	yurak
jaw	jag'
kidney	buyrak
knee	tizza
leg	oyoq
lip	lab
liver	jigar
lung	o'pka
mouth	og'iz
mustache	mo'ylov

neck	**bo'yin**
nose	**burun**
shoulder	**yelka**
stomach	**qorin**
teeth	**tish**
throat	**tomoq**
thumb	**bosh barmoq**
toe	**oyoq barmog'i**
tongue	**til**
tooth	**tish**
vein	**vena; tomir**
womb	**bachadon**
wrist	**bilak**

28. POLITICS

aid worker	**beg'araz yordam ko'rsatuvchi**
ambassador	**elchi**
arrest *noun*	**hibs**
assassination	**suiqasd qilib o'ldirish**
assembly	**majlis**
autonomy	**avtonomiya; muxtorlik**
cabinet	**kabinet**
a charity	**beg'araz yordam beradigan tashkilot**
citizen	**fuqaro; grajdan**
civil rights	**fuqaro huquqlari**
civil war	**fuqarolar urushi**
communism	**kommunizm**
communist	**kommunist**
concentration camp	**konstlager**
constitution	**konstitutsiya**
convoy	**konvoy**
corruption	**korruptsiya; poraxo'rlik**
coup d'etat	**davlat to'ntarilishi**
crime	**jinoyat**
criminal	**jinoyatchi**
crisis	**krizis**
debt	**qarz**
democracy	**demokratiya**
dictator	**diktator**
dictatorship	**diktatorlik**
diplomatic ties	**diplomatik aloqalar**
displaced person	**qochoq**
displaced persons/people	**qochoqlar**
election	**saylov**
embassy	**elchixona**
ethnic cleansing	**etnik tozalash**
exile	**surgun**

free	**ozod**
freedom	**ozodlik**
government	**hukumat**
guerrilla	**partizan**
hostage	**asir**
humanitarian aid	**insonparvarlik yordami**
human rights	**inson huquqlari**
imam	**imom**
independence	**mustaqillik**
independent	**mustaqil**
independent state	**mustaqil davlat**
judge	**sudya**
killer	**qotil**
law	**qonun**
law court	**sud; mahkama**
lawyer	**advokat**
leader	**rahbar**
left-wing	**so'lchi**
liberation	**ozodlikka chiqarish**
majority	**ko'pchilik**
mercenary	**yollanma askar**
minister	**vazir**
ministry	**vazirlik**
minority (ethnic) group	**mayda millat**
minority vote	**kamchilik ovoz**
murder	**qotillik; odam o'ldirish**
opposition	**oppozitsiya; muxolifat**
parliament	**parlament**
parliament *(in Uzbekistan)*	**Oliy Majlis**
(political) party	**partiya**
politics	**siyosat**
peace	**tinchlik**
peace-keeping troops	**tinchlikni saqlovchi quvvatlar**
politician	**siyosatchi; siyosat arbobi**

premier	**prem'yer**
president	**prezident**
prime minister	**bosh vazir**
prison	**qamoq; turma**
prisoner-of-war	**asir**
POW camp	**asirlar lageri**
protest	**protest**
rape	**nomusga tegish; zo'rlash**
reactionary	**reaktsioner**
Red Crescent	**Qizil Oy**
Red Cross	**Qizil Xoch**
refugee	**qochoq**
refugees	**qochoqlar**
revolution	**inqilob**
right-wing	**o'ngchilar**
robbery	**o'g'irlik**
seat (in assembly)	**o'rin**
secret police	**SNB (milliy xavfsizlik xizmati)**
socialism	**sotsializm**
socialist	**sotsialist**
spy	**razvedka; shpion**
struggle	**kurash**
theft	**o'g'rilik**
trade union	**kasaba uyushmasi; profsoyuz**
treasury	**xazina**
United Nations	**Birlashgan Millatlar Tashkiloti**
veto	**veto**
vote	**ovoz**
vote-rigging	**ovoz berishning soxtalashtirilishi**
voting	**ovoz berish**

29. OIL & GAS

barrel	**barrel**
canal	**kanal**
crude (oil)	**xom neft**
deepwater platform	**katta chuqurlikdagi platfo'rma**
derrick	**vishka**
diver	**g'avvos**
drill *noun*	**qazish mashinasi**
drill a well	**quduq qazish**
drilling	**qazish**
exploration	**tadqiqot; razvedka**
fuel	**yonilg'i**
gas	**gaz**
gas field	**gaz maydoni**
gas production	**gaz ishlab chiqarish**
gas well	**gaz qudug'i**
geologist	**geolog**
laboratory	**laboratoriya**
natural resources	**tabiiy boyliklar**
offshore	**qirg'oqdan uzoq; dengizda**
oil	**neft**
oilfield	**neft maydoni**
oil pipeline	**neft kamari**
oil production	**neft ishlab chiqarish**
oil tanker	**neft tankeri**
oil well	**neft qudug'i**
oil worker	**neftchi**
petroleum	**neft**
platform	**platforma**
pump	**nasos**
pumping station	**nasos stantsiyasi**
refine	**aralashmalardan tozalash**

OIL & GAS

refinery	**aralashmalardan tozalovchi zavod**
reserves	**zapaslar**
rights	**huquqlar**
seismic survey	**seysmologik tadqiqot**
survey	**tadqiqot**
surveying	**tadqiq qilish; yer o'lchash**
surveyor	**zemlemer**
supply *noun*	**zapas**
well	**quduq**
well site	**quduq yeri**

30. TIME & DATES

century	**asr**
decade	**o'n yil**
year	**yil**
month	**oy**
fortnight	**ikki hafta**
week	**hafta**
day	**kun**
hour	**soat**
minute	**minut**
second	**sekund**
dawn	**tong payti**
sunrise	**kun chiqish payti**
morning	**ertalab**
daytime	**kunduzi**
noon	**tush vaqti; obed**
afternoon	**obeddan keyin**
evening	**kechqurun**
sunset	**kunbotar vaqti**
night	**kechasi**
midnight	**yarim kecha**
four days before	**to'rt kun oldin**
three days before	**uch kun oldin**
the day before yesterday	**o'tgan kuni**
yesterday	**kecha**
today	**bugun**
tomorrow	**ertaga**
the day after tomorrow	**indinga**
three days from now	**uch kundan keyin**
four days from now	**to'rt kundan keyin**

TIME & DATES

the year before last	**ikki yil oldin**
last year	**o'tgan yili**
this year	**bu yil**
next year	**keyingi yil**
the year after next	**ikki yildan keyin**
last week	**o'tgan hafta**
this week	**bu hafta**
next week	**keyingi hafta**
this morning	**bugun ertalab**
now	**hozir**
tonight	**bugun kechqurun**
yesterday morning	**kecha ertalab**
yesterday afternoon	**kecha obeddan keyin**
yesterday night	**kecha kechasi**
tomorrow morning	**ertaga ertalab**
tomorrow afternoon	**ertaga obeddan keyin**
tomorrow night	**ertaga kechasi**
in the morning	**ertalab**
in the afternoon	**obeddan keyin**
in the evening	**kechki payt**
past	**o'tgan**
present	**hozirgi**
future	**kelasi / kelajak**
What date is it today?	**Bugun chislo necha?**
What time is it?	**Soat necha bo'ldi?**
It is . . . o'clock.	**Soat . . .**

—Seasons

summer	**yoz**
autumn	**kuz**
winter	**qish**
spring	**bahor**

Days of the week

Monday	**dushanba**
Tuesday	**seshanba**
Wednesday	**chorshanba**
Thursday	**payshanba**
Friday	**juma**
Saturday	**shanba**
Sunday	**bozor kuni; yakshanba;** *in Tashkent* **otdix kuni**

Months

January	**yanvar**
February	**fevral**
March	**mart**
April	**aprel**
May	**may**
June	**iyun**
July	**iyul**
August	**avgust**
September	**sentyabr**
October	**oktyabr**
November	**noyabr**
December	**dekabr**

Star signs *in traditional Uzbek order*

Pisces	**Hut**
Aries	**Hamal**
Taurus	**Savr**
Gemini	**Javzo**
Cancer	**Saraton**
Leo	**Asad**
Virgo	**Sunbula**
Libra	**Mezon**
Scorpio	**Aqrab**
Sagittarius	**Qavs**
Capricorn	**Jadyi**
Aquarius	**Dalv**

31. NUMBERS

0	nul
1	bir
2	ikki
3	uch
4	to'rt
5	besh
6	olti
7	yetti
8	sakkiz
9	to'qqiz
10	o'n
11	o'n bir
12	o'n ikki
13	o'n uch
14	o'n to'rt
15	o'n besh
16	o'n olti
17	o'n yetti
18	o'n sakkiz
19	o'n to'qqiz
20	yigirma
25	yigirma besh
30	o'ttiz
35	o'ttiz besh
40	qirq
45	qirq besh
50	ellik
55	ellik besh
60	oltmish
65	oltmish besh
70	yetmish
75	yetmish besh

80	**sakson**
85	**sakson besh**
90	**to'qson**
95	**to'qson besh**
100	**yuz**
200	**ikki yuz**
300	**uch yuz**
400	**to'rt yuz**
500	**besh yuz**
600	**olti yuz**
700	**yetti yuz**
800	**sakkiz yuz**
900	**to'qqiz yuz**
1,000	**ming**
10,000	**o'n ming**
50,000	**ellik ming**
100,000	**yuz ming**
1,000,000	**million**

first	**birinchi**
second	**ikkinchi**
third	**uchinchi**
fourth	**to'rtinchi**
tenth	**o'ninchi**
fifteenth	**o'n beshinchi**
twentieth	**yigirmanchi**

once	**bir marta**
twice	**ikki marta**
three times	**uch marta**
one-half	**yarim**
one-quarter	**chorak**
three-quarters	**to'rtdan uch qismi**
one-third	**uchdan bir qismi**
two-thirds	**uchdan ikki qismi**

32. OPPOSITES

beginning—end	**bosh—oxir**
clean—dirty	**toza—iflos/kir**
fertile—barren *land*	**unumli—unumsiz**
happy—unhappy	**xursand—xafa**
life—death	**hayot—o'lim**
friend—enemy	**do'st*—dushman**
modern—traditional	**zamonaviy—an'anaviy**
modern—ancient	**hozirgi—qadimiy**
open—shut	**ochiq—yopiq**
wide—narrow	**keng—tor**
high—low	**baland—past**
peace—violence/war	**tinchlik—janjal/urush**
polite—rude	**odobli—adabsiz**
silence—noise	**jimjitlik—shovqin**
cheap—expensive	**arzon—qimmat**
hot/warm—cold/cool	**issiq/iliq—sovuq/muzdek**
health—disease	**sog'liq—kasallik**
well—sick	**sog'—kasal**
night—day	**kecha—kunduz**
top—bottom	**ust—tag**
backwards—forwards	**orqaga—oldin**
back—front	**orqa—old**
dead—alive	**o'lik—tirik**
near—far	**yaqin—uzoq**
left—right	**chap—o'ng**
inside—outside	**ichkari—tashqari**
up—down	**tepaga—pastga**
yes—no	**ha—yo'q**
here—there	**bu/shu yerda—u/o'sha yerda**

* This is for formal use only – for a personal friend, use **o'rtoq**.

OPPOSITES

soft—hard	**yumshoq—qattiq**
easy—difficult	**oson—qiyin**
quick—slow	**tez—sekin**
big—small	**katta—kichkina**
old—young	**qari—yosh**
tall—short *people*	**baland bo'yli— past bo'yli**
tall—short *things*	**uzun—kalta**
strong—weak	**kuchli—kuchsiz**
success—failure	**muvaffaqiyat— muvaffaqiyatsizlik**
new—old	**yangi—eski**
question—answer	**savol—javob**
safety—danger	**xavfsizlik—xavflilik**
good—bad	**yaxshi—yomon**
true—false	**to'g'ri—noto'g'ri**
light—heavy	**yengil—og'ir**
light—darkness	**yorug'—qorong'i**
well—badly	**yaxshi—yomon**
truth—lie	**haqiqat—yolg'on**

MAP OF UZBEKISTAN

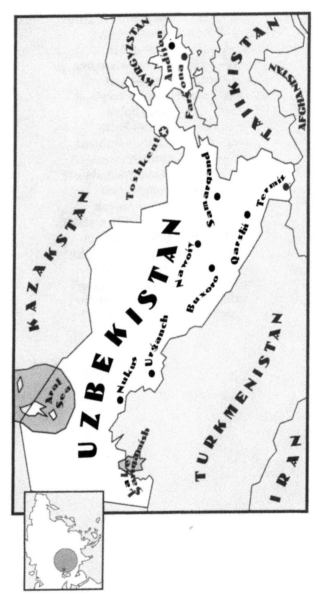